PRAISE FOR THE P

"A masterclass in navigating the high seas of ambition without falling into the whirlpool of overwork and burnout. Mayer's insights empower you to work smarter, not just harder, and to find joy in the journey, not just the destination... A vital compass for anyone who aims to succeed with their sanity intact...a beacon of hope for perfectionists and high-achievers alike."
—Dr. Marshall Goldsmith, Thinkers50 #1 Executive Coach and New York Times bestselling author of *The Earned Life, Triggers, and What Got You Here Won't Get You There*.

"Mayer provides a much-needed deeper dive into the pervasive and unhealthy expectation of perfection, offering highly practical advice for unlearning unproductive perfectionism in work and life"
—Dr. Valerie Young, co-founder Impostor Syndrome Institute and author of *The Secret Thoughts of Successful Women and Men*.

"If you are an ambitious, high-achieving woman, this book will show you how to conquer your inner critic and embrace progress, not perfection. Kathryn provides a supportive guide full of relatable stories and proven strategies that help you to break free of the constant pressure to be flawless."
—Nicole Clopton, Vice President, Head of Learning, GEICO

"The leader of this new era we are entering into needs to move faster and be more agile than ever. Kathryn's book provides a unique toolkit for how to take risks and rebound quickly which our leaders at Women Unlimited have found to be an invaluable resource."
—Dr. Rosina Racioppi, President & CEO at Women Unlimited, Inc.

"Perfectionism is still rampant and a career derailer. Leading a women's professional network, I'm inspired by Kathryn's practical advice and real-people examples of overcoming paralyzing perfectionism. I most appreciate the simple, easily implementable productivity and creativity tools you can use immediately. Crucially, The Productive Perfectionist provides serenity whenever I feel overwhelmed and need a productivity boost!"
—Karen Horting, Executive Director & CEO, Society of Women Engineers

"Conquer your inner critic and embrace progress, not perfection! This supportive guide shares relatable stories and proven strategies for ambitious, high-achieving women to break free from the pressure to be flawless."
—Tasnim Ghiawadwala, Global Commercial Bank Head at Citibank, Kings College, London, UK

"Ditch the self-criticism and celebrate progress with this empowering guide to untangling yourself from the perfection trap. Based on real-life transformations, it's a supportive roadmap for embracing the messy journey towards a more fulfilling life."
—Mike Sebring, Head of Diversity, Equity, and Inclusion, Senior Vice President at Citizens Financial Group, Inc.

"*The Productive Perfectionist* speaks to one of the big challenges women in technology face: even when they become experts, they still struggle to advance. This book offers a roadmap with a lot of compassion and humor. The wonderful stories and case studies of how real women overcome perfectionism kept me delighted. I'm inspired that I, too, can make some tiny changes to play a bigger game."
—Susan Posey, Vice President, Leader, Global Technology Women's Initiative, JPMorgan Chase

"*The Productive Perfectionist* is a great reference for success. Kathryn Mayer's client and personal life experiences and useful interactive tools help us establish a solid foundation to inventory our own strengths and weaknesses and handle our own perfectionist tendencies. A MUST read!"
—Annette Stewart, Senior Director @ RBC | Strategic Business Solution and President of the Financial Women's Association

"Kathryn's vibrant storytelling and user-friendly tools empower readers to break free from self-imposed constraints. I appreciate her accessible coaching style, insightful self-assessments, and practical tools. I wholeheartedly recommend this indispensable book to leaders of ambitious team members grappling with perfectionist tendencies. Moreover, I highly recommend Kathryn as a coach and speaker for companies aiming to enhance productivity and innovation."
—Leo Giglio, Ph.D., Faculty Director, Human Resource Management Program, School of Professional Development, Stony Brook University

"*The Productive Perfectionist*, is an essential book for anyone wanting to learn how to truly be a Productive Perfectionist. Kathryn Mayer has created a clear protocol on how to learn and reflect on our perfectionist tendencies. She delivers a solid evidence-based approach that will revolutionize the way you think."
—Dr. Tammy Wong, CEO of Fostering Executive Leadership, Inc. and author of The Hour Glass Effect

"In leadership development, I've seen the perfectionist story affect a high percentage of people, with a particular vehemence for women. Perfection is a fantasy that blocks access to our real creative power. Kathryn's book shows the path to let go of the fantasy and blossom."
—Bob Dunham, Founder, Institute for Generative Leadership

"More than just "smashing the shackles of perfectionism," Mayer helps you focus on the bigger picture, step out of your comfort zone, and embrace new challenges. Become more self-compassionate, less stressed, as you navigate conflicting demands. Build career success knowing it's ok to make mistakes--and leverage them for your next project. This book makes me more effective as a person, professional, and mother!"
—Zhanna Treybick, CPA, Financial Women's Association Board Member

"Drawing on her diverse experiences as a competitive tennis player, executive coach, and corporate leader, Kathryn provides a unique perspective on perfectionism and how it holds us back. She provides proven practices to overcome your well-established tendencies, push beyond your comfort zone, and win in any field."
—Ann White, Head of New Initiatives and Program-Talent Management, Invesco

"Discover a new perspective in embracing imperfection! "The Productive Perfectionist": a compassionate guide that navigates the complexities of perfectionism, offering actionable insights and exercises for self-acceptance (including fun, real-life examples). A must-read for those seeking liberation from the relentless pursuit of flawlessness. Unlock the path to achieving your goals and embark on a journey toward greater self-awareness and fulfillment.
—Liana Gordon, Director, The Ayers Group

"If you suffer from perfectionism, as so many successful women do (including me!), I recommend reading my esteemed colleague and friend Kathryn Mayer's' new book, *The Productive Perfectionist*. It's full of insight, stories that resonate, and helpful tips."
—Margaret Downs, MBA and Executive Coach, Downs & Associates, LLC

"*The Productive Perfectionist* blends research, personal stories, and practical tools to guide you in conquering your inner voice so you will not just find success, but define it. Anyone in any career, at any life stage, will find it liberating, especially high achievers like my MBA students and the many women I have counseled over the years."

—Anne Weisberg, bestselling author of Mass Career Customization and Adjunct Professor of Management and Organizations, NYU Stern School of Business

"A smart, actionable approach to the paralysis of perfectionism, and its negative impact both on the perfectionist and on the organization. Kathryn Mayer brings her research and leadership experiences (from amateur tennis and finance) to this must-read-and-discuss book. She outlines the concepts of perfectionism through pulse point checks and assessments and shows women how to implement practical steps toward excellence."

—Priya Kaul, Director, Learning Solutions, American Management Association

THE
PRODUCTIVE PERFECTIONIST

A WOMAN'S GUIDE TO SMASHING THE SHACKLES OF PERFECTION

KATHRYN C. MAYER

The Productive Perfectionist by Kathryn C. Mayer

First published by Collaborative Competition Press, 2024

Copyright © 2024 by Kathryn C. Mayer.

ISBN: 978-1-935059-09-7

Cover and interior design by Paul Palmer-Edwards

In memory of my mother, Janet, my first coach. She realized my struggle for perfectionism was burning me out, she constantly challenged me to lighten up. On my last visit with her, as I was struggling to finish this book, she urged me not to give up as the topic was too important. I am eternally grateful for her encouraging words just when I needed them most. Thanks, mom!

CONTENTS

Hula-Hooping on the Roof!

I would never have imagined the pandemic of 2020 would finally free me from my own perfectionism.

If not for the pandemic, I would have published this book in the summer of 2020. I was inches away in March of that year—when the world shut down. Worried that this book, which I'd been working on for five years, would never be published, I was distraught. It was meant to be my platform to launch a new business. Suddenly, I had lost control of my future. All I saw was deep uncertainty.

My body felt tense and heavy. I called my publishing consultant, Shel, and asked what he thought we should do. He said, "An eBook will be a great way for you to smash your shackles of perfectionism. Write it in twenty to thirty hours, and we'll get it on the market quickly." This conversation made me more anxious. I have never written a book in less than five years, and he wanted me to do it in just a few months?

Shel's insight that the crisis could be just the opportunity I needed to free myself from perfectionism led me to realize my real worry about publishing an eBook without years of review and editing: It could be crap.

Could the pandemic be my chance to face that old lurking fear of not being good enough without a lot of preparation? My preference in tackling new things is to go step-by-step, practice and practice until I feel confident. Instead, I had to move fast. It seemed that everyone was just adapting as they went. The old standards of success were on hold or just gone.

Once I could step back and see that the new normal projected "I don't know," I felt permission to throw stuff against the wall without worrying that it might ruin my reputation. But for me to enter this new world of experimentation, I needed to lighten up and get into a positive mood.

So, I dusted off my old pink Hula-Hoop and began a new routine of hooping every day on the roof of my Manhattan apartment building. As I started to lighten up, I understood that what I needed most was to increase self-care.

In the new COVID-conscious world, most people seemed paralyzed and unsure. But when I was Hula-Hooping on the roof, I felt silly and playful. Staying in that fun mood of lightness when I was afraid to leave the house would take deliberate and focused intention. In the pre-COVID world, I would squeeze little bits of self-care into the corners of my life. But in the early days of the pandemic, I needed to organize myself around it. The new organizing principle felt foreign to me and made me even feel a little guilty with so much death and bad news everywhere. But did the world really need more depressed people? As I Hula-Hooped, I discovered that I not only *could* get out of my own way—I *had to* if I really wanted to help others.

Shel's timetable was too far out of my comfort zone—but why not challenge myself to create a new eBook in six months? I was part terrified and excited. I decided to test the idea. I took a deep breath and sent an email to my network to recruit fifteen to twenty self-proclaimed perfectionists who would participate in a complimentary pilot program to survive and even thrive in the strange "pandemic world."

Much to my amazement, twenty freaked-out professionals from nineteen to seventy years old signed up. Then, of course, I had to create and teach the model. It would be based on the book I'd been writing for five years—that you're reading right now—but also weave in the new, terrifying challenge of COVID and make it integral to the project.

Shel was right. I didn't have the luxury of overthinking and continuously refining. As I reworked the ideas, I'd typically finish the modules just minutes before each meeting. I was always nervous as each session started, wondering if my ideas would resonate and be useful.

The program involved developing, teaching, and discussing the four SANE steps to thriving during a crisis:

Small steps. Break both the fight-or-flight, freak-out reaction and the perfectionist paralysis—"I can't do it perfectly, so I won't do it at all"—enabling you to move faster.

Accelerate experimentation. Develop comfortable new ways of working, so you can expand your options, increase innovation, and enhance results.

Nurture. Practice self-compassion, humility, and the idea that you and others can still grow—all of which help you recover more quickly from mistakes.

Exercise your network. Ask people you trust for more stretch feedback and support than you would in normal times.

My pilot group and I met twice a month for two months on Zoom. During each seventy-five-minute session, my goal was to create a safe and open environment. I began each session by sharing my foibles and challenges and encouraged everyone else to do the same. I taught one of the SANE skills, and then we explored ways that each person could weave new thinking into the fabric of their days and weeks.

I watched and listened as people moved from their initial freak-outs to become calmer and more compassionate with themselves and each other. The focus on self-care allowed the members to become bolder; each reached out and asked for what they wanted. For example, one of the women in the group, Deborah, had lost her job. She started reaching out to a wider group of people through LinkedIn, asking for an introduction to someone they might know within an organization at which she was applying for a job. Previously, Deborah hadn't been that assertive.

We were all experimenting and improvising together. The surprise finding from my pilot program was that increased self-compassion was the biggest takeaway. My old fear-based catastrophizing cycle of thinking—if this program doesn't go well, then my clients won't hire me, and I will end up a bag lady—was not happening. In fact, the opposite was occurring. The more each of us shared our humanity and humility, the more space we left for others to do the same.

I published the eBook, *How to Stay SANE and Successful in the COVID World,* in six months. It was imperfect. I found a sizable mistake in the first edition, and we had to revise and publish it again. But I just kept going. This freedom bled into my tennis game. I started playing more highly ranked players, losing more but getting braver, and, eventually, beating better players some of the time.

This newfound confidence on the tennis court is significant because this is where my perfectionism began. I grew up as a top-ranked junior tennis player, and my identity became tied to my latest win or loss. This led to decades of struggle with performance anxiety on the tennis court, rooted in fear of losing. I realized if I could survive publishing an imperfect book, creating on the fly, and doing something I would have previously thought impossible, I can rebound from losing a tennis match, too. I no longer see my achievements and slip-ups as self-defining.

Now, here we are, three years later. I feel as though I am languishing, in transition from the COVID world to whatever the next normal turns out to be. Some of us have entered the Live-Only-for-Today Economy. We are stepping back and asking questions like:

- What now?

- What do I care about?

- What life do I want to live—what does the life of my dreams look like?

- Do I want to go back to my old life?

- If not, what would I change?

- How is my perfectionism holding me back from that imagined ideal life?

I realize I am no longer the same person I was in early 2020. My comfort zone has expanded beyond that perfectionist I once embodied. I've learned how to:

- Move faster

- Ask for help sooner

- Learn from mistakes and move on

- View experimenting as a valid and enjoyable way of life

A wonderful tingly, light feeling has replaced the perfectionist heaviness and anxiety. I'm no longer letting my life be dominated by fear of mistakes. I no longer obsessively worry that I am always one step or loss away from disaster. Now I know I can handle whatever shows up. *And even if it's not perfect, I can recover.* My new standard of success involves experimenting and moving faster. My expanded comfort zone gives me more choices: Do

I want to speed up, or is it worth it to go slow and step-by-step?

It is a choice, not a chain wrapped around my neck.

Trying to figure out this new normal, I started attending conferences on the future of work. At a Financial Women's Association event in March 2021, the keynote speaker, Ida Liu, the global head of Citi Private Bank, began her talk with "Don't be a perfectionist" if you want to grow you career. She said women tend not to stretch outside of their comfort zones and don't take on new roles unless they are one hundred percent qualified. In contrast, Ida credits her own meteoric career rise because she kept taking on roles for which she wasn't qualified and stretched into them.

With so much uncertainty around us, we need to rethink what productivity and success look like. While we may feel less in control—which is tough for us perfectionists—we are still in control of our choices. I offer this book, *The Productive Perfectionist: A Woman's Guide to Smashing the Shackles of Perfectionism*, as a tool to help you step back and reflect on the mindsets and tactics that will empower you to work in a whole new way. Perhaps it could be your personal golden ticket—your chance to free yourself of the chains of perfection and create a way of working and being that will tingle and inspire.

INTRODUCTION

The people you'll meet in this book are former coaching clients, participants in training or coaching engagements, or women who partook in the two virtual coaching pilots of The Productive Perfectionist. Their names have been changed.

Meet the cast of characters:

Amy, a new mother and high-potential insurance professional. She wants to be taken seriously and advance in an organization with only male leaders.

Bart, **Dina**, **and Dan**, all colleagues working on a trading desk at a global financial service company; Dina, a young mother with two small children, struggled with how to be self-promotional as a woman in a male-dominated world.

Bethany, who works in a large bank's technology group and wants to become a managing director.

Betsy, a finance executive and self-proclaimed perfectionist who moved from successful money manager to COO at a large global bank, and **Dave**, her boss.

Carol, who came from a small town and moved to New York City with a big job in real estate and needed to learn to navigate the male-dominated world of real estate development.

Chris, a manager who doesn't want to retire, and **Sara**, a finance executive who reports to Chris and is grappling with his reluctance to step away.

Christine, a dedicated nursing executive who rarely took time out for herself.

Tiffany, a high-potential woman leader who is newly engaged and trying to lighten up.

Clare, a general counselor who lost her job after her boss was let go.

Daria, a newly promoted leader in the fashion industry who has a brilliant sense of style but struggles with communicating effectively.

Elizabeth, a human resources executive and self-described perfectionist who wants to use the ideas in the book to lead a team—and maybe even to get her children to clean their rooms.

Faye, a single, working mother in a male-dominated business, looking for ways to assert herself at the office.

Fiona, a new nursing executive in a large hospital, working under **Jill**; the two had opposing styles, and Fiona needed to learn how to manage Jill to be successful in her new role.

Jane, a former teacher and single mother of two children who rose to become a C-suite executive for a Fortune 500 financial services company.

Jo, a nonprofit executive who rarely took time for herself.

Joan, a lawyer who works in finance but felt uninspired at work.

Joe, the CEO of a small financial services company.

Pierre, the manager of several coaching clients and a senior executive at a global financial services company.

Sabrina, a successful trader for a large global financial services firm. She loathes networking but wants to get promoted to managing director.

Sally, a lawyer with two young children who works in finance. She struggled with how to exercise her creative side.

Sheryl, a woman leader in her late fifties who had given up on playing tennis because she saw herself as not good enough.

Stevie, a finance executive and perfectionist in her mid-fifties who was looking to get her mojo back.

I'll offer stories from our characters along with examples of how they have broken free from the shackles. My aim is to inspire you to take action as part of a supportive community.

This book provides a road map to replace the small, anxiety-ridden life of a perfectionist with a free-spirited, joyful one. You may find that you become happier, less anxious, more self-compassionate, enjoy greater control and increased choices, engage in taking more small risks, develop a clearer vision, rebound from mistakes more quickly, and enjoy your successes more.

And, if you are interested in more after reading the book, you'll discover many options to participate in small group and individual coaching, and join an online community.

What other results might you expect?
You will:

- Learn that you are not alone.

- Discover tools that will help you evaluate what risks to take, your approach to getting out of your comfort zone, and how to rebound safely from slip-ups.

- Overcome feelings of failure or being an imposter as you become more self-compassionate, resilient, and confident.

- Learn why self-compassion is the quickest way to become more productive and how to practice it on a daily basis.

- Break through the panic or flight-or-fight reaction to successfully start new habits by taking very small steps.

- Learn how to ask for help and gain the feedback and support you need to achieve your goals and make achieving your goals easier.

- Learn how to manage others' unrealistic demands and expectations—in your career, family, and life—so you're energized and productive, rather than overworked and drained.

- Participate (at your option) in a community on social media that provides support, encouragement, and opportunities to form new relationships.

CHAPTER 1

The Perfectionist Dilemma: Why it Matters for Women

"Perfectionism is the voice of the oppressor, the enemy of the people. It will keep you cramped and insane your whole life."[1]

—Anne Lamott

Perfectionism is the true gender ceiling. Women strive for perfection. But men view perfection as situational. While striving for perfection appears noble, it actually weakens women's positions.

How often do you ask yourself questions like these?

How come I seem to be working harder than everyone, but I don't receive the recognition or promotion I deserve?

How am I supposed to fail fast and still do a good job?

Who has time for networking and schmoozing with the boss and senior executives?

How do I deal with team members and managers who have unrealistic expectations?

How come those people apply for a new role or better job when they're NOT qualified?

How am I supposed to stay on top of everything when I have a long to-do list?

Why am I experiencing little satisfaction and joy with all that I am accomplishing?

How do I keep from burning out?

If these kinds of questions keep coming up, this book is for you!

Reading *The Productive Perfectionist* will break you out of the trap of working too hard while still not getting fair recognition. You'll build the right relationships, so you're not going it alone. You'll learn how to take career risks and rebound with grace. And you'll learn how to "fake it 'til you make it." The result? You'll feel more self-compassion, work smarter —and yes, even have some fun along the way.

A typical perfectionist

Betsy always prided herself on striving for perfection. This strategy helped her move from successful money manager to C-suite executive. Betsy and her boss, Dave, the division's president, had worked together fairly effectively, delivering strong financial returns.

Dave became frustrated with Betsy. She seemed to take an eternity to finish some tasks. He'd asked her to review the compensation plan for a group of employees she supervised and come back with some quick recommendations. Months passed with no update. Dave wondered what was taking so long. He even gave Betsy permission to hire a few more people to reduce her workload. He was beginning to question her judgment.

Despite Dave's desire for a quick win, Betsy worried whether doing things well and quickly would be good enough. As she started reviewing the compensation plan, she found numerous, serious issues. She believed nothing short of a complete overhaul was warranted, but her boss wanted information and action right away. Betsy viewed his request as an opportunity to impress by going beyond expectations. She started working late and over the weekends.

As Betsy's coach, I shared that during my monthly check-in with Dave, he'd expressed frustration with her slow rate of work. Betsy looked shocked. I asked Betsy if she and Dave had ever agreed on a definition of "winning." Betsy said no. She believed her boss wanted her to do the best job possible. But for Dave, winning meant speed, not perfection.

Betsy was aiming for perfection when her boss really wanted "good enough." Compounding the problem, she believed asking for help would make her look weak. In contrast, Dave was trying to be a good boss by offering to take something off her plate. Betsy's judgment was clouded by striving for perfection—she couldn't see that her boss was questioning her credibility as a senior executive. For Betsy to succeed in her new role, she needed to learn a new approach to productivity. Don't worry. There was a happy ending, and I'll share it near the end of the book.

Why perfectionism limits your productivity in the 21st century

Perfection is critical for doctors, accountants, aviators, and engineers—professions in which mistakes can be fatal. But when you constantly strive for perfection, it becomes a problem. For example, Dave expected flawless financial statements but could overlook imperfections if the compensation plan came fast. Often, good really is enough; spending that final twenty percent won't yield a better outcome.

Perfectionism limits your success and enjoyment of life

Perfectionists link their identity to accomplishments, continuously seeking affirmation that they're good enough. Otherwise, they feel like imposters and failures—depressed and insecure. They avoid taking risks. They can't take rejection. They'll put their heads down, study, practice, take lessons, and get advanced degrees with honors. They pass the CPA exam but don't become partners. They try out for a Broadway show and give up after one rejection. The list goes on.

What's the new strategy for success in the 21st century?

What's great about perfectionists is that they care about doing things well and want to be productive. Key synonyms for "productive" include effective, industrious, and practical. As a perfectionist, I see two other possible synonyms that some might equate with productive: profitable, focused on the bottom line; and gratifying, focused on the process. But therein lies the conflict. Perfectionists strive to achieve or exceed standards. But, like Betsy, they often work too slowly, missing the big picture or pushing themselves too hard. In contrast, focusing on the process means better results through the creation of a supportive environment.

So, what does productive mean in the 21st century? Doing great work is no longer enough. Both *quantity* and *quality* are critical. Even perfectionists must learn to complete only seventy-five percent of some tasks and not spend the extra effort to achieve one hundred percent.

Wharton Business School professor Adam Grant, in his 2016 book, *Originals*, says the trade-off between quantity and quality is false. Research shows new ideas increase quality. But many people fail to generate new ideas because they're too focused on perfection.[2]

In an article in *The New York Times Magazine* by writer Adam Davidson, "Welcome to the Failure Age!", Davidson said, "We're now in the age of constant invention, which begets constant failure. Innovation's lifespan has never been shorter; most new products last just a few years, or less. To harness this new age of failure, we have to quickly bounce back from mistakes."[3]

Why do women need a strategy to succeed in the 21st century?

I've spent over twenty-five years working in talent management roles—half the time as an executive coach and the other half in highly competitive global firms, including Goldman Sachs and Deloitte. I've worked with thousands of women in the United States, Canada, the United Kingdom, Europe, South America, the Caribbean, and Asia.

And everywhere I go, typically seventy to ninety percent of women admit to being perfectionists.

"The typical firm experiences a fifteen percent increase in profitability when it goes from having no women in corporate leadership to thirty percent female representation," according to a study of twenty-two thousand companies by the Peterson Institute for International Economics.[4]

Yet, in today's world, to grow your career, expand your business—or just continue to be employed in the modern world—you need to get comfortable taking risks. Perfectionism can hold you back and limit your options. For example, research shows when men and women are applying for new jobs, women will often only apply when they have one hundred percent of the qualifications—while many men feel they only need fifty percent, according to CNBC's Jennifer Openshaw.[5] With this pattern, women will always be staying "small."

Why do I care about this topic?

I, too, have played the "small" game.

I grew up passionate about tennis. I started playing at nine years old. I enjoyed practicing for hours, taking lessons, and welcoming the challenge of competition. As a tall nine-year-old at five foot nine inches, I used my height to win tournaments by running to the net, waving my racket around, and scaring little girls. When I was thirteen or fourteen, my tennis coach pointed out that because the other girls were growing taller, I would need to change my strategy to keep winning. This would involve staying at the baseline and becoming a more consistent and patient player. I would probably have to lose a lot in the beginning. I can remember thinking, "Why should I do that? I am winning. I don't want to become a loser. How would I stay motivated?"

I told him, "No, thank you," and became a very good doubles player, building upon my serve and volley game. This decision still pains me.

The pain isn't that I feel like I lost my chance to be the next Billie Jean King. Rather, I let my fears shrink my goals and lost all joy for the sport. As a perfectionist, I couldn't see how I could scale back without losing my self-confidence.

I can attribute my perfectionism to many factors: DNA, upbringing, dysfunctional family dynamics, inept coaching, and gender. My mother's motto was that if you were going to do something, you must do it well. This meant that she wanted me to take weekly, private tennis lessons and play in tournaments to sharpen my skills, even though we could only afford half-hour lessons.

I'm grateful that my mother valued coaching; it has allowed me to enjoy everything from skiing to public speaking to drawing.

But none of my coaches ever taught me *how* to take the risks and manage the necessary setbacks. Adding to the problem, my father was an academic neurologist who worked all the time, set a high bar for achievement, and offered little positive feedback. I felt torn as a little girl. I wanted to please my mother by becoming an accomplished tennis player. But my father rarely, if ever, watched me play or supported my tennis achievements. In this perfect storm, I became a perfectionist who never felt good enough and defined herself by her achievements. After suffering from severe anxiety and panic attacks in tennis matches, I decided that there must be another way.

I was determined not to let my striving for perfection hold me back. I wanted to live large. But I realized I needed to take small steps.

What this book is...
This book shows perfectionists how to create a safe environment even when they work in unsafe organizations. It will provide insights on what type of risk-taker you are, what your comfort zone looks like, how to create a positive emotional climate, and how to build productive and supportive relationships. You will learn how to break that risk-takers block and take that first very small step. It will build your confidence to make better choices in your career and life and help you feel less anxious, more compassionate, and joyful.

What the book is not...
The goal of this book is not to eliminate perfectionist tendencies. Perfectionism has positive aspects; it's part of your personality and helped you get where you are now. This is not a psychology book

that will diagnose you or offer a prescriptive cure; the bibliography offers a lot of good resources.

It's also not a time management or project management handbook. Again, I've listed good books to help you manage your time and your life. This book will empower you to manage your career and life in the 21st century, which requires both teamwork and constant stretching outside of your comfort zone. And if you want additional support, I offer various group and individual coaching options at the end of the book.

Who is the target audience—and what's the goal?

If you want to grow your career and/or get more comfortable taking smart risks at work and in your life, this book is for you.

The main elements for success are:

- Curiosity and a willingness to learn and grow

- The deep urge not to live too small—to have an impact

- A desire to live a more joyful, less anxiety-ridden life

The book is for people of all ages and from all walks of life and levels of education, people in business, government, nonprofits and community organizations, and academia; those who get paid or volunteer, work in an office, in the field, or from home. Women between the ages of twenty-five to eighty-five will tend to gain the most. Anyone who is ambitious and has perfectionist tendencies will benefit.

CHAPTER 2

Where Does Productive Perfectionism Come From?

"If you think that caring for yourself is selfish, change your mind, because you are simply ducking your responsibilities."

—Ann Richards, governor of Texas, speaking to
the Michigan Menopause Action Team, September 23, 1999

D o you often feel like you are not good enough even when it looks like you're doing an amazing job and living a high-quality life? This book can be a virtual hug, helping you accept who and what you are and finding strength in the things that try to knock you down.

I know about productive perfectionism—because I've been there.

Over the past thirty years, I've participated in cognitive behavioral therapy, coaching, and support groups from Toastmasters to the Five O'Clock Club. I've read innumerable self-help books encouraging women to take risks, such as *Lean In* and *The Confidence Code*—and others encouraging everyone to jump in, such as *Fail Fast, Fail Often* and *Think & Win Big*. These books teach building confidence by preparing for—and rebounding from—failure.

For example, *The Confidence Code* has a chapter, "Failing Fast and Other Confidence-Boosting Habits," that lists tactics, such as "stop seeking permanent praise or ruminating about that mistake and move on."[6] But these aphorisms feel trite and oversimplified to me. Why can't I jump on that failing-fast bandwagon?

None of these books provide a step-by-step approach to actually creating a life of smart risk-taking. This book and my virtual training program, also called *The Productive Perfectionist*, offer a SAFE strategy for risk-averse perfectionists—teaching *how* to "lean in." Please go to my website at www.kcmayer.com to sign up for the program.

Blending disparate ideas from positive psychology, sports psychology, risk-taking mindsets, networking strategy, organizational savvy, Heart Math, Japanese *kaizen*—or using very small steps to improve—and ontological coaching—the science of living—I've created one cohesive model. The goal is to help perfectionists overcome risk-averse tendencies and become more productive. When you need speed, I give you a plan—and when you err, I can accelerate your recovery.

What I learned from women who piloted The Productive Perfectionist virtual coaching program

When I began this journey, I expected that women wanted help increasing their influence or making some bold career moves. But when I conducted two virtual coaching pilots to test out my risk-taking strategies for perfectionists, my mentees wanted something deeper. These two pilots were run over two three-month time periods between 2015–2017. One pilot included five women and the other, seven; each had four modules that ran for seventy-five minutes.

Let me share a story of how letting go of perfection transformed one woman's life

Faye, a single working mother, joined the program because she worked in a male-dominated environment—and, as a self-proclaimed perfectionist, she never felt good enough. She felt lower in confidence compared to her male colleagues. She began the pilot program to feel more joy and confidence in her life.

After the first session, which focused on building a positive emotional climate, she realized that she wasn't very compassionate with herself. She adopted an affirmation: "I will be supportive of myself, no matter what." This led her to take a half day off to attend an event with her daughter. In the past, she would have forgone the event, fearful of being perceived as a woman who takes time off for her children.

Faye realized she held numerous negative views about herself. The small group helped her work through a list of positive attributes for which she'd received accolades at work and in life. As she reflected on this list, she recognized she has a lot to offer but has been beaten down. She understood that being with her daughter brought her joy. The surprise was that taking time off for herself built her confidence. She felt energized and came back to work feeling empowered.

The following week, her boss gave her feedback that she'd handled a complex project well, despite a few errors. She repeated her affirmation before she met with him to review the mistakes. This allowed her to feel self-compassion—not self-doubt—as she corrected the errors. Self-compassion turned out to be her critical takeaway. This new practice led her to apologize less and feel more self-assured at work.

When Faye and I had a follow-up conversation three months later, she had successfully detached over the Christmas holidays and enjoyed time with family and friends. This small step of practicing self-love provided the way out of a joyless and perfectionist-striving life.

I share Faye's story and others throughout the book. The anecdotes offer examples of a common perfectionist belief that if you can't take a big step, why bother? This belief becomes a vicious cycle. To counteract that attitude, *The Productive Perfectionist* teaches habits that are small enough to do every day. Similar to overcoming writer's block, you just need to get started. You've got to play to win!

Key learnings from the pilots

Perfectionists want support around a wide range of activities. They want to:

- Manage and reduce their guilt about wanting to enjoy their life and not let work consume all their time

- Learn to be more compassionate toward themselves

- Reduce their stress at work and in life

- Make a career change

- Find the courage to get comfortable speaking up in a male-dominated environment

- Build a stronger, high-performing team

- Realize that they are not alone

CHAPTER 3

How Perfectionism Limits Your Career and Life: Five Key Actions to Breaking Free

"Striving to be perfect creates a negative mind-set in which you're bothered by every little thing that goes wrong, since even a small mistake can 'ruin' the whole. And negativity is never valued in a leader."

—Sally Helgesen and Marshall Goldsmith, in *How Women Rise*

Striving for perfection as an approach to managing one's career can limit your options and success. The book *Why CEOs Fail* offers this list of the perfectionist's main beliefs and actions.[7] How many do you see in yourself?

- Want to do the best job possible

- Need to be in control, i.e., be involved in every step

- Link their successes and failures to their identity

- Try to do everything themselves, have trouble saying "no" and/or delegating

- Are unable to see the big picture, stuck in the details

- Spend an inordinate amount of time on secondary tasks instead of the strategic or long-range issues

- Focus on enhancing efficiency and short-change the impact on people

- Avoid taking risks in which they don't see immediate or possible success

- Resist celebrating the latest victory out of fear that they may not be able to live up to it

- Believe that anything less than perfect is mediocrity

Perfectionism decreases career success and enjoyment

When I review this list with groups of high-potential women, most of them tend to raise a hand on over fifty percent of the list. If you see yourself in many of these bullet points, then you, too, may suffer from perfectionism.

As a result, your activity at work and in life becomes focused on maintaining perfection and avoiding failure, rather than what's good for you personally or professionally. Many people, including me, developed a perfectionist approach early as a child.

I was praised for *winning* my tennis matches, rather than for my effort. My identity became my latest win or loss. This limited self-definition led to performance anxiety and resistance to growth. Thus, I didn't grow as a tennis player. This same pattern plays out with many people I coach. They don't want to apply for their bigger job or make a presentation because they are afraid they might fail.

Perfectionism and the growth mindset

Perfectionism creates a fixed mindset: the belief that your qual-ities—such as math or athletic ability—are carved in stone. This belief tends to bring about an urgent need to prove over and over again that you can do math or play a sport. This concept comes from *Mindset*, a book by Carol Dweck, a world-renowned Stanford University psychologist who has done decades of research on achievement and success.[8]

Dweck's twenty years of research has shown that the view you adopt for yourself profoundly impacts the way you live your life. She has discovered that those who have a growth mindset—the belief that you can improve through your own efforts—tend to thrive when things are not going well. While people do differ in their innate talents and interests, she shows that everyone can enhance the ability to play a sport or learn a new skill. Dweck cites many examples: Ben Hogan, one of the greatest golfers of all time, was uncoordinated as a child. Cindy Sherman, one of my favorite photographers and one of the most important artists of the twentieth century, flunked her first photography course.[9]

I find it fascinating that Dweck says women have a harder time adopting the growth mindset due to our perfectionist tendencies. She talks about how little girls grow up trying to please and trusting too much in people's opinions. For example, I gave up on math in middle school after years of high achievement because one teacher said I lacked aptitude in geometry. This is why perfectionism and the fixed mindset are so shackling. It makes it very difficult to thrive and rebound during difficult times. As women, we tend to give too much credence to other people's opinions of us. Often, our challenge turns out to be learning to trust ourselves and relish the rewards of growth.

Dweck's book is an excellent read for those wanting to go within and build the growth mindset.

In contrast, this book works from the outside in—to allow us to break out of the perfectionist trap by taking small actions.

Breaking out of the perfectionist trap

Your colleague at work gets the promotion that you have been working towards for the last year. You are very disappointed. You attempt to get a cab home, but they are all taken due to bad weather. Uber is charging surge prices, and the subways are experiencing delays. You finally get home and realize you lost your favorite gloves. You attempt to share the news with your husband, but he isn't listening; he just found out his mother may be dying.

How do you handle a bad day?

In 1996, Daniel Goleman published a groundbreaking book, *Emotional Intelligence*, which confirmed that success in life is based more on our ability to manage our emotions than on our intellectual capabilities. His research helps explain why many individuals with a high IQ may not do as well in life as those with higher emotional intelligence (EQ).[10]

The HeartMath Institute builds upon Goleman's work.[11] Its research has shown that when the heart is engaged, it can lower blood pressure, improve nervous system and hormonal balance, and facilitate brain function. For the mind and emotions to perform at their best, the heart and brain must be in harmony with one another. Heart intelligence is the insight that can be experienced once the mind and emotions are brought into balance. Negative emotions throw the nervous system out of balance and leave it in a chronic state, stressing the heart and other organs—which can potentially lead to serious health problems. In contrast, positive emotions increase balance in the nervous system and produce smooth, harmonious heart rhythms. The result: reduced stress and a more optimistic perspective. The good news is that EQ can be developed over life. One of the fastest ways to get into a positive emotional state is to take small actions. HeartMath has found that as little as five minutes a day of gratitude thinking can make a huge impact.

Gratitude is a strong antidote to perfectionism. It is one of a few key emotions that can break the negative thinking pattern.

How to handle the bad day with a HeartMath approach

I go into my bedroom, close the door, put on my calming head-phones, and write—first, how I feel; second, what I am grateful for. If I feel like crying, I will do that too. I might read a few pages from my success journal to remind me of past accomplishments. Then, once I felt calmer and more positive, I would return to reality.

What is critical to breaking the perfectionist trap is getting out of your head and into your body.

Faking it until you make it

Another practice that builds upon emotional intelligence and HeartMath is Amy Cuddy's research on the power of making small tweaks in your body to change how you feel.

Most people believe that emotions happen first before physical sensations—that our minds cause most of what we feel in our bodies. In other words, I play tennis because I am happy, not I am happy because I play tennis. Research has proven that this common belief is often incorrect. In reality, we can feel sad because we cry or afraid because we tremble. Feelings can be either a consequence or a cause of emotional behavior and bodily responses. Sometimes, our bodies respond to emotions with physical reactions like tears, laughter, or trembling—but at other times, we can laugh or dance our way out of a dark mood. [12]

Amy Cuddy has popularized this research and made it accessible all over the world. If you haven't watched Amy Cuddy's 2012 TED talk,[13] which has been one of the most-watched videos in the world, or read her book, *Presence*, I would encourage you to do so. Amy shares her story of being in a car accident at seventeen years old, suffering a traumatic brain injury, and losing thirty IQ points. She dropped out of college as an honor student. Her doctors told her she wouldn't finish college. Yet, she became a Harvard business school professor. How did she do it?

Through a slow, painstaking process.

The imposter syndrome is normal

Cuddy learned to make small tweaks in her behavior: faking it until she became more confident. This faking-it concept is similar to imposter syndrome—also known as impostor phenomenon or fraud syndrome —a term coined in 1978 by clinical psychologists Dr. Pauline R. Clance and Suzanne A. Imes, referring to high-achieving individuals who can't internalize their accomplishments and have a persistent fear of being exposed as a fraud.[14] In contrast, Cuddy prefers to name it "imposter experience"; she believes it's fairly universal.

Recent research has found that both men and women experience the syndrome in equal numbers.[15] Wikipedia lists Sheryl Sandberg, Sonia Sotomayor, and Albert Einstein as having said that they felt like imposters. Valerie Young, the author of the book, *The Secret Thoughts of Successful Women: Why Capable People Suffer from the Imposter Syndrome and How to Thrive in Spite of It,* acknowledged that she decided to focus on women because chronic self-doubts hold women back more than men.[16] Whether women are held back more by their own beliefs, by stereotypes, or systematic obstacles, you can use your body to overcome these self-limiting beliefs.

Cuddy's 2012 TED talk describes Power Posing—standing in a Wonder Woman pose for two minutes—before engaging in a challenging activity. Her research demonstrates how holding a simple posture for two minutes increases testosterone and reduces cortisol. The testosterone fires you up while lowering cortisol calms you down. While some recent research challenges the validity and reliability of her work,[17] HeartMath's studies support the concept that even spending tiny periods of time in a positive emotional state can have lasting impact.

I am one of millions of people around the world who have benefited from the Power Pose. I used the two-minute Wonder Woman pose before giving a keynote speech in front of over a thousand people—going into a stall in the restroom to do it. This simple action simultaneously helped me override my freak-out instinct and energized me. I felt calm and confident even though negative thoughts of "don't screw this up" danced in my head.

Cuddy has received thank you notes from a wide range of people who have used this tool for everything from preparing for a job interview to playing the violin at Carnegie Hall.

Two key foundations for smashing the perfectionist shackles

As you can see, tiny steps are the keys to building new habits and smashing those shackles. The concept of taking these small risks comes from two well-tested practices:

Practicing the ancient Japanese technique of kaizen (continuous improvement in small, incremental steps). Japanese corporations have long used the gentle technique of *kaizen* to achieve their business goals and maintain excellence. Your brain is programmed to resist change. But by taking small steps, you literally rewire your brain so it bypasses the flight-or-fight response and creates new connections so that you can move rapidly towards your goal.[18] For example, when I was starting this book project, I believed that I needed to write for one hour a day. But even though I'd already written an earlier book, after a whole year, I had barely written anything.

When I attended a writing workshop to jump-start my book, my instructor suggested that I aim for thirty-minute writing shifts three days a week. This was doable. Another year later, I finished the first draft of the book. Once I started to build in the habit of writing, I found ways to increase it and make it happen regardless of my schedule.

Taking small physical actions. Research demonstrates that five minutes of deep breathing or two minutes of Power Posing can reduce stress in the body and help to manage your emotions versus letting them manage you.[19] The goal is to build new sensations in the body that are lighter, more expansive, and full of oxygen—and that will eventually override the tight, heavy, and constrained feelings of perfectionism.

Moving from actions to habits

Given that we perfectionists are busy, I've narrowed Productive Perfectionism down to five actions—a simple roadmap to get you out of your comfort zone with less stress.

These five actions are each meant to be done five minutes a day. You can do them separately, build upon one another, or do all five at the same time.

Five actions of Productive Perfectionists

- **Build a positive emotional foundation.** Harness three positive emotions—joy, gratitude, and compassion—to keep perfectionism from overwhelming you. Learn and implement the daily practices that lower stress and increase productivity.

- **Strive for the situational win: excellence instead of perfection.** Set your definitions of accomplishment within each specific situation, both for yourself and for your team. This approach helps you make progress on your goals, adapt quickly to change, and enjoy your life overall.

- **Learn how to evaluate what risks to take and rebound safely from slip-ups.** Understand your approach to getting out of your comfort zone; take steps to make risk-taking simpler and rebounding faster.

- **Create a safety net of trusted relationships.** Learn to be vulnerable in select ways—such as asking for help and giving credit—so you can build trust more quickly and increase comfort with risk-taking.

- **Lighten up! Get rid of limiting "shoulds,"** such as, "I should have a clean house." Instead, create empowering new mantras such as, "I can hire a housecleaner and accept that it will be clean enough." Identify and implement at least one activity that encourages playfulness. It could be Hula-Hooping five minutes a day, taking a singing course, or committing to any other passion that brings joy outside of work achievements—and results in more creativity, innovation, and productivity.

Actions turn into habits once you repeat them enough

There are a lot of myths about how long it takes to form a new habit. I used to believe it was twenty-one days, but recent research has found that on average, it took sixty-six days—more than two months. The range was wide: from eighteen days—say, to drink a bottle of water with lunch every day—to two hundred fifty-four days to start running twenty minutes a day, five days a week.[20]

So don't expect everything to be perfect, especially at first. You need to give yourself permission to make mistakes, to slide back to old ways—to perfect the new habit over time and not all at once. It's totally normal to feel like you are faking it 'til you make it—because you're starting as a newbie. Every top achiever started as a clumsy beginner. Even the superstars in sports, arts, science, business, and every other field had to learn how to do it.

You can't grow without some discomfort. Remember the first time you rode a bike—you probably fell down. A core driver of success is to learn how to be kind to yourself so you can bounce back more quickly. We'll provide opportunities for you to break out of those actions that keep you shackled and build in some rewards so that these new actions become habits.

CHAPTER 4

Productive Perfectionism Self-assessment: Examine Your Comfort With the Five Actions

"I think self-awareness is probably the most important thing toward being a champion."

—Billie Jean King, tennis star, in *Sportswoman*, November/December 1973

Becoming self-aware is the foundation for improvement. You can't change that of which you are not aware. To gain clarity on where to focus, take the Productive Perfectionist Self-assessment. The twelve questions explore ways that the chains of perfectionism may be holding you back—and how many ways you're already breaking free of those shackles. Your overall score will determine whether you are:

- An Unproductive Perfectionist

- A situational Productive Perfectionist

- A Productive Perfectionist

Remember: as a Productive Perfectionist, your goal is to be able to do things well, take risks, rebound quickly, manage the expectations and demands of others—and enjoy the process!

- Take the self-assessment, and identify a numerical score. Your answers will reveal your comfort (*not* skill) in practicing these core five actions.

- Review your results and develop an action plan.

- Use your overall score to determine where you are on the scale between Unproductive and Productive Perfectionist. **The goal is to move from unproductive to productive.**

- Identify those areas in which you feel comfortable practicing and those you want to enhance. Where are you strong? What actions need increased practice to become a habit?

- Remember, the results do not measure skill, they measure frequency and comfort.

- Keep in mind the goal is to identify the strengths you can build upon and those one to two areas you could benefit from performing more often.

The Productive Perfectionist self-assessment

This assessment is designed to determine if you are a Productive or Unproductive Perfectionist. Take a moment to reflect on how you think and act—both at work and in life.

Rate yourself honestly on a 1–10 scale. Answer the questions quickly, and spend a second or two on each. Your score provides you with increased self-awareness about your perfectionist tendencies so that you can improve.

Reflection	Scale		Your Score
1. How much do you worry about achieving 100% in everything you do?	(1) Even small, mundane tasks must be accomplished perfectly. →	(10) You immerse yourself in the things that really matter but work much less intensively on the rest.	
2. When you approach a project, do you set clear goals or standards of excellence for both yourself and your key stakeholders?	(1) You assume your key stakeholders will accept nothing less than perfection, so you push yourself to achieve that. →	(10) You gain agreement on achievable goals, clear standards, and small milestones to celebrate along the way.	
3. How often do you find yourself feeling grateful?	(1) You only feel or express gratitude when it is deserved. →	(10) You feel continually grateful for what you have. And you actively seek opportunities to thank people every day.	
4. How often do you practice a self-compassionate approach?	(1) You tend to be tough on yourself. You believe that your best results will come from working hard. You push through losses and tough times. →	(10) You habitually speak to yourself in a kind and non-judgmental way. You view your weaknesses as ways you can improve; you aim to learn from your mistakes.	
5. How do you bounce back from a mistake or a setback?	(1) You see your mistakes as permanent personal failures that undermine your ability to handle the situation. You actively look for ways to minimize your exposure in the future. →	(10) You're resilient. You attribute the mistakes to specific causes, honor your strengths, and feel optimistic about where you can improve so you can avoid making the same mistake in the future.	

Reflection	Scale		Your Score
6. How often do you spend time in pure enjoyment—such as hobbies or spending time with friends/loved ones?	(1) You engage in enjoyable activities only when your work schedule allows. →	(10) You regularly build in time for enjoyment. Even when busy, you'll take five minutes to listen to a favorite song or call a friend.	
7. How often do you look for opportunities to make people look good—such as offering compliments or giving credit?	(1) You almost never give credit unless it is fully deserved. →	(10) You frequently seek out opportunities to make people look good—you feel that helping others is a smart strategy.	
8. How often do you appropriately make yourself vulnerable—such as asking for help or admitting a shortcoming?	(1) You rarely make yourself vulnerable. You believe that you have more leverage when people view you as confident and not needing assistance. →	(10) You are comfortable asking for help or admitting a shortcoming when appropriate.	
9. How often do you ask for a push and/or constructive/positive feedback from key stakeholders or your support team?	(1) You seldom ask for constructive or positive feedback. You assume people will offer feedback when you need it. →	(10) You realize that to improve your performance, you must regularly ask for positive and constructive feedback.	
10. How often do you seek assistance or suggestions on your projects—and from whom?	(1) You hardly ever ask for assistance; you prefer to do things on your own. →	(10) You regularly seek out a variety of partners whose diverse backgrounds, areas of expertise, and views challenge your perspective.	

Reflection	Scale		Your Score
11. How often do you focus on building and maintaining relationships with the 10-15 key stakeholders in your network?	(1) You don't have time for networking; you are too focused on doing excellent work. →	(10) You consistently engage in a variety of activities, ranging from helping your key stakeholders to having lunches or attending events that expand your network.	
12. How do you define yourself?	(1) Your self-definition is linked to high and rigid standards, or "shoulds." You feel shame or heaviness if you don't live up to your ideals in your personal and/or work life. →	(10) Your self-definition comes from accepting your strengths and imperfections. You're able to adapt to changing circumstances, such as age, interests, or feedback.	
13. How often do you find ways to engage in playful activities?	(1) You don't believe that spending time in playful activities, such as Hula-Hooping, singing along with the radio, or coloring in an adult coloring book, are a good use of time. →	(10) You understand that as a perfectionist, you tend to be too serious and need to remind yourself to lighten up. Thus, you regularly find time to integrate playful activities, even if it's just for five minutes at a time.	

Scoring

The Productive Perfectionist involves five key actions:

- Building a positive emotional foundation.

- Striving for the Situational Win instead of perfection.

- Learning how to evaluate what risks to take and rebound safely from slip-ups.

- Creating a safety net of trusted relationships.

- Lightening up!

Your answers to these questions demonstrate your level of comfort with these core behaviors. You can interpret your numerical scores in a couple of ways:

- Review your answers based on the topic areas, or

- Total your scores. If you review your answers both ways, you can easily identify the areas where you're doing well—and those where you're too caught up in perfectionism.

Topic areas

- Questions 1–2 focus on striving for the Situational Win instead of perfection.

- Questions 3–6 focus on positive emotions along with rebounding from slip-ups.

- Questions 7–11 focus on forming and maintaining a safety net of trusted relationships.

- Questions 12–13 focus on lightening up.

Numerical scores

13–49: you lean toward *Unproductive* Perfectionism. You often aim for perfection more than satisfaction. You avoid risks or reaching out and asking for help unless it's absolutely necessary. While you might occasionally feel satisfied, feel able to determine what risks to take, or successfully get support, too often, you try to power through alone and then resent yourself for failing.

50–85: you're a *situationally* Productive Perfectionist. Sometimes you feel satisfied. Other times, you tend to be more of a perfectionist. It's important to recognize when you feel satisfied and where you need to develop new habits to achieve more situational wins, feel more positive emotions, gain more support, and loosen up. Your goal is to be consciously competent.

86–130: you're a *Productive* Perfectionist. You consistently focus on going for the Situational Win, and frequently feel grateful, satisfied, and joyous. You understand your need to take risks. You put in the effort to grow, actively build up your resilience, regularly seek out feedback from a variety of people, and don't take yourself too seriously.

Steps to becoming a *more* Productive Perfectionist

- Identify one area in which you are already productive: a strength you can build upon. This would be any question that you answered 5 or above.

- Identify one area where you are unproductive: an area where you can grow or expand. This would be any question in which you answered 1 or 2.

- Identify why you want to make this change. It is important to have a driving care or reason. Ask yourself, "For the sake of what will I change?"

- Identify a thirty-day plan to add a new habit to your repertoire.

For example, your staff complains that you push them so hard, they get demotivated. A star performer even quits, citing your hard-driving behavior as a key reason. How do you begin to change your behavior?

Perhaps you want to work on becoming more compassionate and less hard on yourself and your staff. You could begin by establishing a goal to become more compassionate with yourself and others for the sake of improving the team's performance and the company's goals.

You make a new declaration that you will say to yourself every morning. The declaration could be something like, "I will act compassionately toward myself and others—for the sake of bringing out the best in my people."

Your goal is to tune into what you care about and use those insights to create a clear direction for your behavior.

Then you can share a new way of working together with the team. You want people to feel safe asking questions or making mistakes. You will meet with people who report to you directly to learn how you can make them feel comfortable bringing up issues or concerns. Meet weekly, review this approach with them in thirty days to determine how things are progressing, and continue to use their feedback to adapt your approach.

CHAPTER 5

Action 1: Build a Positive Emotional Climate

"The HeartMath Institute has done substantial research and found that just spending five minutes a day in appreciation lowers blood pressure and cortisol (the stress hormone), boosts the immune system, and elevates serotonin (the mellow hormone) levels for up to ten hours."

Doc Childre and Deborah Rozman, *Transforming Anxiety: The HeartMath Solution for Overcoming Fear and Worry and Creating Serenity*[21]

In this chapter, we will look at how you can build the three core positive emotions—gratitude, compassion, and joy—as the antidote to perfectionism and develop regular practices to bring more of these key emotions into your life.

For many years, the idea of spending time being grateful only seemed relevant when I'd accomplished something of significance. Otherwise, it seemed like one of those silly new-age truisms.

That changed after I was fired by a ruthless leader at a women's empowerment nonprofit. At first, I felt like I'd lost faith in humanity and in myself. Although I'd worked at investment banks where I had experienced many a Machiavellian who would do anything to win, she caught me by surprise. I felt shame—how could I have ended up here even though I viewed myself as a savvy, experienced professional? I also experienced grief at my lost future, helping women in developing countries, and anger that the board of this organization allowed this woman to repeatedly bring in new people, use them, and then fire them. It was overwhelming.

But my coach at the time encouraged me to do two things:

- Focus on having self-compassion

- Start a gratitude practice each morning for at least five minutes

She said the people in this world who are the happiest are also the kindest to themselves and the most grateful. While this made sense, it was still very challenging for me to forgive myself and to find more than a few things about which I could feel gratitude. The same short list kept reappearing—my supportive husband, a nice apartment, and a few good friends. Little by little, this tiny habit started to give me courage to move on and to share my disappointment and to begin the journey to what was next. I now begin every day by writing down ten things for which I am grateful. And I've learned to find different things to list every day.

This tiny habit continues to snap me out of my negative funks. It also surprised me that greater self-compassion was one of the most common benefits from my two Productive Perfectionist coaching pilots. The women, all self-proclaimed perfectionists, realized that being hard on themselves wasn't helping.

Having self-compassion is foundational. If you want to become more productive, you need to learn how to be self-compassionate, be grateful, and find some joy. You need to have your own back. Otherwise, you risk staying too small. Your negativity limits your thinking—and thus your options.

So, if you tend to focus on how the leader in the group didn't seem to listen to or acknowledge your contributions, then you can quickly start feeling resentment. But, if you can stay more self-compassionate, you might find yourself looking around the meeting room and noticing that others are silently smiling or supporting your views. And this observation could prompt your curiosity to follow up with these people after the meeting and explore their views and see if you can gain their support in the future. Just by supporting yourself, you increase your options exponentially.

Understand the three key emotions: gratitude, compassion, and joy

The following chart on emotions describes the underlying thoughts and feelings for the three core emotions and shows simple ways you can weave them into your life. The goal is to provide several examples of tiny steps you can take to break out of Unproductive Perfectionist thinking and actions. The three stories in the case studies that follow illustrate how these feelings help you become more creative, re-energized, and productive.

Emotion	Thoughts and feelings	Practices
Gratitude	Be thankful for things that have happened without any effort. The more you think and feel gratitude, the more life feels juicy and ripe with possibilities. Thoughts of gratitude include thanking people who have helped or supported you. Feelings include appreciation, peace, warmth, generosity, connectedness, and optimism.	• Take small, regular actions. Begin each day by listing five to ten things for which you are grateful: health, home, a beautiful day, and so on. • When something good happens unexpectedly, thank the person responsible. • Send someone a thank-you note. • Say a heartfelt thank-you to all the people you see regularly—from the mail delivery person to the grocery store clerk. Look the person in the eyes, smile, and add something personal—such as how much you appreciate their friendly attitude.

CartoonStock.com

Emotion	Thoughts and feelings	Practices
Compassion	Talk to yourself in a kinder and gentler way, so you can learn from and correct mistakes. Stay curious about a challenging situation; don't negatively judge yourself for making a mistake. Thoughts include talking to yourself as you would to a friend in need of help. Feelings include kindness and gratitude toward yourself, giving yourself a break, and being generous with yourself.	Talk to yourself before, during, and after taking risks and feeling challenged. • Before you enter a new or scary situation, tell yourself that you will love yourself regardless of the outcome. • During events, quietly recite a phrase or focus on an image that calms you down or makes you laugh. For example, when I'm giving a presentation in front of a large audience, I keep telling myself, "I have wisdom that they want to hear." Or you can always follow the advice given to beginning speakers to imagine their audience in their underwear. • When you are with people who push your buttons or whom you don't like (or in any other uncomfortable situation), tell yourself to stay curious: What can you learn here? What parts of yourself are feeling annoyed? For example, I struggle with people who talk nonstop and don't ask questions; they make me feel like maybe I am not smart enough. So, I have an internal dialogue with myself, encouraging myself to speak up and not take this personally. • After a setback, talk to yourself in a gentle and understanding manner. Research shows that people who viewed their weaknesses from a self-compassionate perspective were more likely to see them as changeable. And this increased their motivation to improve and avoid the mistake again.[22]

Emotion	Thoughts and feelings	Practices
Joy	Cultivate joy by celebrating certain situations, such as an accomplishment—or you can just choose to celebrate life. Thoughts of being pleased with yourself or events—and wanting to celebrate. And your belief that doing activities that bring joy are critical to your well-being. These activities could include spending time with family and friends, playing a sport, seeing a movie, or planning a vacation. Feelings include gratitude, appreciation, happiness, peacefulness, being in the flow, and enjoying the moment and activity for its own sake.	Three types of activities that can increase joy in your life. • Taking the time to celebrate small and large victories. This could mean an anniversary, birthday, or an accomplishment. • Including an activity that you do just for the pure enjoyment every day and each week. Daily activities could include having a cup of tea, taking a ten-minute walk, or calling a friend. For weekly activities, perhaps something more challenging: participating in a sport or going to the movies with friends. • Allow some room for spontaneity and doing nothing. We perfectionists tend to be doers, leaving far too little time to just be in the moment and experience life. Try allowing an hour a week— just ten to fifteen minutes a day—to sit and do nothing.

Case studies on compassion, joy, and gratitude

Sara found compassion during a tough leadership transition

Sara, a coaching client, shared how she is struggling to deal with her retiring boss, Chris. Sara is a warm, relationship-oriented communications professional, groomed by Chris to take over his division upon his retirement. But when Chris wouldn't retire gracefully, the company planned to force him out within a year's time.

Sara was disappointed to hear that Chris would not help her with the final phase of learnings during his last year. She felt discouraged, as she would have to quickly figure out how to do Chris's job without his help. Mistakes would be made, things could fall through the cracks, and worse, she could fail. Sara had always looked up to Chris; suddenly, she struggled to find compassion for him.

Sara had to be versatile enough to be firm yet kind with Chris. She also felt forced to do something she hates: ask senior leaders for help. Sara viewed herself as assertive and considerate—but she questioned whether she could find the balance.

This situation threatened her view of herself as a consummate professional—always planning, working well with others, doing a great job, and making very few mistakes. After all, Sara was accustomed to cleaning up Chris's mistakes, taking a back seat, and rarely, if ever, asking for help. She had never considered that always striving for perfection and being hard on herself was holding her back. This awareness was the first step to accepting that if she wanted to thrive as a more senior leader, she needed to become more self-compassionate. She might not be able to find empathy for Chris, but she had to accept that she could not control his actions. She could only control herself.

We tried a variety of experiments to help Sara cope. One that worked well was practicing thinking on her feet to get her accustomed to accepting inconsistencies, being open to possibilities, and learning to be nicer to herself. One of the exercises that helped build this muscle was the improvisation game, "Dr. Expert," which involves answering ridiculous questions in a credible manner. For example, "Why do mosquitos who wear skin-tight bathing suits fly faster than those who don't?" The goal is to practice sounding credible about topics with your body language and tone of voice.

Sara began this exercise with slumped body language, many "ums," and a soft voice. Yet, she had very credible answers. She was quick to speak but was concerned about coming across credibly.

First, I reminded her to lighten up. We were talking about mosquitoes! Once she realized that she could pause and just give herself a break, she started speaking more confidently, not worrying about small mistakes. We then expanded this experiment to practicing the answers to work-related questions and asking for help. This helped Sara realize that if she practiced self-compassion, she would be able to handle whatever Chris could throw at her.

Most of us have a story of how we want to be seen. What helped Sara accept the challenge of this situation was realizing that she wanted to take on this bigger role for the sake of building a strong team and helping others to grow. To succeed in this bigger role, she would need to grow too. She would need to communicate more assertively. And she'd have to ask for help from her superiors. Once she let go of being perfect all the time, she was able to ask the senior executives to help manage Chris *and* help in her transition.

The A-ha Moment for Sara was discovering that feeling like a fake is perfectly normal as we begin to make changes. It means we're willing to try new behaviors to find out what's right for us in a new situation. The more compassionate and playful we can be with ourselves (rather than have the fist in the back)—the sooner the desired result will be achieved.

Why bother finding joy in a busy life?
The indomitable Katherine Hepburn said, "If you obey all of the rules, you miss all of the fun."[23]

"We need to struggle. We need to organize. And we need to dance." This is how Debora Spar ends her book on women and perfectionism, *Wonder Women: Sex, Power, and the Quest for Perfection.*[24] She believes that, somehow, joy fell out of the equation of all the benefits that a life of choices should bring—more joy, not less. So, here is the former president of Barnard College, one of the most prestigious women's colleges in the United States, advocating that women choose joy as an important criterion for success.

Martha Beck wrote an excellent book called *The Joy Diet.*[25] The first habit in Beck's book that tends to get overlooked is, "Make room for spontaneity and doing nothing." I think it's critical advice for those of us with busy, overscheduled lives.

Indeed, spontaneity taught me a lesson about joy when a vacation went awry.

I never wanted to go to Uruguay. My dream was to go to Rio De Janeiro. My husband thought Uruguay sounded interesting based on a 2014 *The New York Times* article. I agreed to Uruguay if we could spend half the time in Rio.

We got to the airport and gave the agent our tickets. She asked for our visas. My husband, who did all the organizing for the trip, looked stunned. My husband is very detail-oriented, thorough, and fastidious. He said, "You have to be kidding me. I bought the tickets and have been talking with ticket agents and tour guides. No one mentioned that we have to have a visa to go to Rio!" The ticket agent said, "Sorry, but we can't let you on the plane without it." She cancelled our tickets and said we could reuse them another time.

I was about to cry. We grabbed our bags and found a seat in a nearby café. "What are our options?" I was ready to strangle him. My husband is an experienced traveler who understands the visa issue, having traveled extensively on business to China and other developing countries. How could he have missed this detail?

We started trying to figure out what to do. How much money had we lost? How much more would we have to spend to go anywhere else?

But there was another feeling arising: The thrill of an adventure.

Over the previous month, I kept hearing about this beautiful resort area in Uruguay: Punta Del Este. First, from my young Argentinean hairdresser, who said all the hip young people go there to party. And second, from a client of mine who had spent a lot of time there and said that the beaches were gorgeous—white sand, fabulous restaurants, and a relaxed, crime-free environment.

My husband doesn't tend to look to his young hairdresser as the source for planning last-minute vacations, though. And we don't do beach vacations. But, given the unusual circumstances, my husband was relieved I had a plausible idea. Still, he suggested Panama or somewhere else in South America that doesn't require a visa.

We returned to the ticket agent and explored options. Given that we already had tickets from Uruguay to New York, we thought why not just spend the entire vacation in Uruguay? However, as it was pre-Christmas, there were only two tickets left to Uruguay from New York for the following night—for an additional one thousand dollars each. On impulse, we took them and headed to Miami that night.

I finally started crying in Miami over the loss of going to Rio. My husband, too, was terribly disappointed at the loss of all his hard work, money, and planning. We talked it through, had a couple of cocktails in South Beach, and the world started to seem pretty good. The next day, we started looking online for a place to stay in Punta. We found an amazing spa with an indoor hot tub, sauna, outdoor pool, near the beach, located in a charming neighborhood—for around one hundred and fifteen dollars a night.

Punta was amazing. It was so sunny, quiet, easygoing, and relaxed. I settled right in. Having traveled to other South American countries such as Colombia and Argentina, I was accustomed to having armed guards and pickpockets everywhere. But Punta was nothing like that. It was full of parakeets, white sandy beaches, charming restaurants, art galleries, and a variety of unique neighborhoods—including one called Beverly Hills, with one-acre plots and multimillion-dollar homes.

My surprise was that, although I still wanted to go to Rio, it seemed like Punta and Montevideo were a perfect respite for my husband and me. We walked the beaches, I read a light book called *The Night Circus,* and fell in love with the two circus performers, Widget and Poppet, swam in the refreshing water, enjoyed the long days (the sun set at nine each night), and ogled at the gorgeous sunsets. My favorite memory was going to the Casa Pueblo designed by the famous Uruguayan artist Carlos Páez Vilaró and watching the sunset. It is a Uruguayan tradition that while the sun sets, you hear a poem read in Spanish about the sunset.

Somehow this whole trip felt more energizing than others because we had to improvise, and we didn't know what was going to happen. My life in New York City is so busy and focused on constantly planning and scheduling that it felt so refreshing to wing it and be open to possibilities. The A-ha for me was that I realized I need more of this spontaneity in my life. I have a lot of freedom and creativity in my work life as a coach, facilitator, and trainer. But I don't leave enough space for improvisation; I am constantly *doing*. The trip was about *being*.

Given that I'm a perfectionist in recovery, I'm a bit of a pessimist. I often become fearful if there isn't a plan. My mind goes to the ten things that might go wrong. This trip reinforced the idea that life can be lived and enjoyed without a plan.

The learning for me was to leave space for dreaming, for doing nothing, for wandering, for not having a goal every minute of every day. I came back from that trip reenergized and looking forward to making time for just being. How is that for a new goal? And I am even becoming more of an optimist.

Jo learned how a gratitude practice energized her

Jo, the president of a nonprofit organization, joined The Productive Perfectionist pilot. Driven and a hard worker, she doesn't take a lot of time off or often do things for herself. She joined the pilot as an opportunity to do some self-care.

Jo realized during the first module that she could make at least as much progress with small steps. She began a gratitude practice on the way to and from work. Walking to work, she reflected on what she was grateful for in life—cute dog, good relationship with her parents, young husband, and an apartment in her favorite city. On the walk home, she'd reflect on her day and identify something good that happened. She also reviewed what didn't go so well and what she could do differently. This simple regular gratitude practice led her to feel more energized in general and clearer about big decisions at work.

Creating a practice

Now that you understand compassion, joy, and gratitude and the value of having them in your life, you need to start a regular practice. It's called a practice because it's something you do repeatedly with the intention to learn something new. It is how we develop skill, competency, and knowledge.

At first, it will feel awkward. Mistakes may happen. But practiced enough, it becomes a habit and skill. More is better. You can do it every day. What makes the change sustainable is making it a habit. That's where being a perfectionist helps—because we love to work hard. Remember, even if it might feel too easy, give it thirty to sixty days. Engage in your practice every day for thirty days. If you miss a day, no big deal; just start again the next day. This habit is about having your back.

We perfectionists miss an important truth about productivity. We think it's all about hard work. That's an excellent foundation, but it's not enough to keep growing personally and professionally. When you regularly make a little time for gratitude, self-compassion, and joy, your subconscious starts to know that you've got this. You can stretch, take risks, and get back up again without berating yourself. I know some of you may still be suspicious, because it seems too easy. I felt that way too, as did Jo and others. Give it a chance. The thirty-day trial. Let's continue the journey to the next action.

Shackle-smashing actions

Learn to build new feelings and sensations in the body to feel so much lighter, more expansive, and full of oxygen that these joyful feelings will override the tight, heavy, and constrained feelings of perfectionism. What one small step can take your perfectionist "shackles" off?

Here are several examples.

- Make a bold declaration, such as, "I am good at being compassionate toward myself. I support myself no matter what happens." And say it whenever you need it during the day.

- Make time to attend a yoga or Pilates class once a week or as often as your schedule allows. Aim for success; if you can only attend once a month, start there.

- Create one small physical action to break out of those shackles. On your walk home, for instance, reflect on what went well and where you could improve; talk to yourself compassionately.

- Listen to your favorite song for five minutes between meetings.

- State simple, daily mantras in the morning or at lunchtime: "I am grateful for my job." Research has proven that these simple mantras can make you feel happier.[26]

- Spend five minutes every morning, listing ten things for which you're grateful.

CHAPTER 6

Action 2: Striving for the Situational Win Versus Perfection

"If somebody can do something eighty percent as good as you think you would have done it yourself, then you've got to let it go."

Sara Blakely, founder of Spanx, *Marie Claire*, interview November 4, 2014

Striving for perfection is draining and unproductive. This is because perfection is tough to achieve and can take a long time, which is not always ideal—or even desirable.

At the beginning of the book, I shared the story of Betsy, who was aiming—slowly—for perfection, when her boss, Dave, really wanted "good enough"—and he wanted it quickly. To achieve perfection, Betsy had to exceed her boss's expectations and work overtime. But for Dave, winning meant getting the project done faster rather than perfectly.

They had differing ideas on the Situational Win.

One of the most important things a perfectionist needs to learn is to pause and ask what the Situational Win looks like. Situational Wins involve gaining agreement on what conditions will satisfy both the individual carrying out the task and the other key stakeholders. Situational Wins reduce anxiety. The clarity they provide increases productivity and effectiveness.

Dave's idea of a Situational Win had been to make only a few changes to the compensation plan in year one, and implement other reforms in the future. Once Betsy realized that there was a lack of agreement on the final goal, she was able to clear it up with her boss and complete the project. Betsy also had an A-ha moment: She needed to start trusting Dave's intent more and ask questions, instead of assuming the worst. And Betsy needed to realize that she couldn't do everything herself, and Dave expected her to ask for resources to help her finish the report.

This core habit can help you learn to take smart risks more comfortably. How do *you* define a Situational Win? What do your clients, boss, husband, or key stakeholders care about? How do *they* define winning?

To distinguish between perfectionism and the Situational Win, review the following charts. And explore an example from professional tennis that helped me understand the value of defining satisfaction and celebrating the small wins.

Striving for the Situational Win Versus Striving for Perfection

	Thoughts	Emotions	Actions
Perfectionism	Rigid standards; Must be 100% Fear of failure Never good enough Distrust/negative view of situations and people who don't share similar views Pessimism	Anxiety Resignation Resentment Anger Relief if things go well	Always striving for the perfect result based on your view of the world Protecting your views—and becoming defensive or depressed if things don't work out Avoiding risk; you don't try a new activity unless you can be sure it will succeed Judging, whining, or attacking other's views Rarely taking the time to celebrate or be grateful
Situational Win	Aiming for the best result for you and/or other key stakeholders in your environment. The focus is on gaining agreement on the standard for success. Acceptance of yourself regardless of the outcome Assumed innocence or good intent Optimism Good enough Courage	Confidence Gratitude Joy Compassion Acceptance Acknowledgement Satisfaction	Conversing with yourself and those you work with about gaining agreement on the conditions of satisfaction and acceptable outcomes Recalibrating and practicing resilience if things don't work out Celebrating big and small wins

Distinguishing Perfection from the Situational Win

PERFECTIONISM		SITUATIONAL WIN
Feeling never good enough	Versus	Striving to achieve a certain specific end goal

The satisfaction habit: double satisfaction

I want to underscore this point with a professional tennis example: Doubles tennis is my favorite sport to play and watch. At the professional level, it's a very fast-moving game that involves strategy, partnership, strong volley skills, and, much to my surprise, a lot of focus on creating a positive emotional climate.

Leander Paes was one of the world's greatest doubles players, winning ten Grand Slam doubles titles. A few years ago, I watched him lose a tough third-round doubles match at the US Open. What's interesting to watch, along with Paes's quick feet, sharp angles, and crisp volleys, is what happens on the court between him and his partner.

The pattern looks like this: After each point is completed, the pair "high-fives" and has a brief ten- to fifteen-second chat, and then they return back to their respective places on the court. This pattern happens after every point—win or lose—with constant communication and acknowledgement of effort. There isn't usually a louder hand slap over a huge win or fussing over a badly played point. I've never seen negative emotions between the two. Occasionally, you will see one of the pair yell, "Come on" to himself or slap his leg after a mistake. What is amazing to me is that after watching them play for over two-plus hours in extreme ninety-degree weather and lose 6-2, 4-6, 6-1, their pattern between points never wavered.

I became curious. When I started watching more professional doubles matches during a recent US Open, I noticed that most teams practiced a version of this pattern. It seems to be an industry best practice—a satisfaction habit. Slapping hands after each point—win or lose—is a deliberate, physical way of acknowledging satisfaction. Granted, tennis is a sport. But taking the time to acknowledge satisfaction is not common in sports, or in life overall, unless one tends to win. The physical act of hand-slapping appears to keep the team in a positive, or at least neutral, mood, leading to an emotional feeling of satisfaction (versus anger or joy), so they can figure out what to do next. It is critical during any competition or challenging business situation to stay in a mildly positive or neutral state; otherwise, the risk of becoming too angry or elated can cloud the ability to observe and analyze the situation.

This approach comes from Jim Loehr, a performance psychologist, and best-selling author. He observed tennis players and found that those players who managed the sixteen-second break between the points effectively were able to tolerate more types of stress and recover more quickly to achieve full performance. The players who took the time to reflect, speak about what went wrong to themselves or their partner, visualize a future positive outcome, and then take some small action—such as high-fiving their partner or moving their racquet from their left to right hand between the points—are more relaxed and play better.[27]

So, how can you apply this habit in your everyday life? Learning to feel satisfied is the first step for perfectionists or anyone suffering from feeling less-than. Celebrating satisfaction will create more of a positive emotional state—which, research shows, will calm down the nervous system and help produce patterns of thought that are more unusual, flexible, and better apt to lead to more creative actions.[28]

Three years ago, a tennis partner asked me to play in a small local women's doubles tournament. My first reaction was "no." As a perfectionist, I didn't feel ready to win. My partner convinced me that she was fine with any outcome and just wanted to play it for fun. Although I was afraid to make a fool of myself, I entered my first doubles tournament in twenty-plus years. I thought it would be a good opportunity to stretch and help me play better tennis. Practicing the satisfaction habit helped me stay positive or neutral when I wasn't playing well and avoid moving towards that place of self-doubt— "What was I thinking?" I was able to stay somewhat relaxed as my partner and I did high-fives after most points, which contributed to me playing better. I was able to find more creative doubles strategies beyond just hitting the ball over the net. Much to my surprise, we won!

How you can practice the art of satisfaction in your life

Newfield Network lays out three steps to determine your Situational Win when coordinating action for yourself and with others.[29] (I'll describe the Newfield Network coaching program in more detail in the chapter titled Building a Safety Net). I learned this approach during my coaching certification in 2012 and have been using them ever since: future action and conditions of satisfaction; making clear what we want (future action) and what standards will be acceptable (conditions of satisfaction). This approach can be used for both individuals and groups/teams.

Practicing satisfaction really worked for me
in a match with my doubles partner.

In tennis, the future action might be to play the best we can regardless of the outcome and the conditions of satisfaction would be to high-five each other—win or lose. At work, an example might be, "Can you send me a draft of the new business card by tomorrow at noon?" It is important to agree on specifics, voice your concerns, and declare yourself a beginner if you are unsure about the end product.

For instance, if you are hiring someone to update your website, and you have no knowledge of how to do this, it is important to share that. Another simple example would be when you don't like your current haircut, but you aren't sure what type of new hairstyle you desire. When you visit a new hairdresser, the conditions could be to share that you don't like your hair so short but aren't sure what might be better.

Also, be clear on the time frame. When do we want others to do what we want them to do? Sometimes it is obvious—and other times, it's not. What "as soon as possible" means to one person may be different from what it means to another.

After an action is complete, declare satisfaction—then celebrate or recalibrate. It is critical to actually state to yourself and/or the others involved that you are satisfied. It's important to tell yourself that you are satisfied regardless of the outcome. The following steps are aimed at helping you and others bounce back more quickly when you are aiming for a Situational Win. These steps can be used for individuals and with groups.

- **Celebrate.** Take some small physical action. Walk, dance, or listen to your music while walking. Just as the tennis players' physical action between the points helps to calm them down and create a positive emotional climate, taking action will calm you. At work, you might give a colleague a high-five after completing a task, or plan a celebratory dinner after completion of a big project. This builds the belief that you are good enough, regardless of the outcome.

- **Recalibrate.** If you didn't finish your task, you need to recalibrate and identify one specific reason why you didn't complete it or why it didn't go as well as planned. Like the doubles players who talk between points, you need to tell yourself that while you usually can do this task, there was a specific reason why you did not. State this reason verbally or write it out. Then, like the tennis players, high-five or acknowledge your effort regardless of the outcome—and move on. Successful workers and athletes learn from their mistakes and have a short memory.

- **Repeat.** The more often you can do this the better. Remember: The tennis players do it after *every* point—win or lose. Start small. Try it once a day and then gradually increase. You'll begin to reap the benefits of positive or neutral emotion. You have a much better chance of winning the second time around or deciding to try something different if you come from a place of positive or neutral emotion.

An example of a satisfaction habit

Elizabeth, an HR executive, joined my pilot group as a self-described perfectionist. I asked participants to read my blog posts along with articles about the topic. During the second module, focused on satisfaction, Elizabeth read the story of how professional doubles tennis players do high-five slaps after each point—whether they win or lose. Elizabeth, not being a tennis player, was excited about this idea and decided she would try it with her team. She asked her team members to start high fiving each other's efforts and achievements. These small steps energized her team and increased morale. The success led Elizabeth to ask, "Can I do this at home with my children? Maybe I can get them to help out more around the house or clean their rooms."

This is why a small satisfaction is so important to productivity: It energizes people and improves morale. Let's help you create your own satisfaction practice.

Exercise #1: Find more proyour pink hula-hoop

My favorite way to celebrate small wins is to dance to my favorite music with a big, pink Hula-Hoop that came into my life during an Omega Institute rest and relaxation weekend. Women from Hooping Harmony[30] were Hula-Hooping and selling brightly colored hoops. Before that retreat, the last time I'd attempted to Hula-Hoop was while visiting my nine-year-old niece. The hoop was barely wider than my hips, and, needless to say, after one or two hulas, it spent most of the time by my feet while my niece enjoyed laughing at me! At Omega, I realized how much fun and joy can be had from five simple minutes of dancing or hooping. Now, when I am working from home, and I finish key tasks, I Hula-Hoop for two minutes.

The goal is to develop a habit of learning to feel satisfied for making the effort and/or achieving something every day. Here are possible exercises to experiment with every day:

Define your conditions of satisfaction. If you write a to-do list every day, make note of which tasks are both important and urgent, important but not urgent, or not important. Add time frames, or determine what must get done in the present day. I like to tackle the hardest tasks first.

Reward yourself. Give yourself a two-to-five-minute reward when you complete the task.

What are your conditions?

Decide how you want to declare satisfaction. It is imperative to acknowledge (even in a small way) that you've completed the task.

Rewards could include:

- Listening to your favorite music

- Dancing to your favorite music

- Hula-Hooping

- Walking around the floor or around the block

- Getting a cup of tea

- Texting or calling a friend

- Engaging in any activity you enjoy

How will you celebrate or acknowledge your results?

Practice talking to yourself using the emotions of gratitude, compassion, and joy. "I feel satisfied because I did my best."

"I am compassionate with myself and recognized that I wasn't at my best today because I didn't feel well."

"I feel grateful that I had the opportunity to interview for the job, due to my friend's connection."

What will you say to yourself?

Moving towards satisfaction and optimism

I begin each day by taking fifteen minutes to figure out what critical things need to get done, how long they'll take, and how I'll celebrate when I've finished. The hardest day of the week for me is Monday—but not because it is Monday. It's challenging because Monday morning is my time for getting organized, and there always seems like there's too much to do. So, I have to work at not feeling overwhelmed and stuck. The first step I take is making the list, and then I figure out how long things might take.

The other big challenge I face is that I struggle with being realistic about how long things will take. I just assume I can do everything quickly. I hate to admit that I can't do something within the allotted time. Why? Because then I won't feel good about myself.

Ironically, it's my perfectionism that creates unrealistic time frames. I still must work at accepting that my second draft will be good enough, and I don't need to go back and polish half a dozen more times. But I've learned to accept that even my perfectionism isn't perfect. Like Betsy, I can get a task completed, resist the urge to keep tweaking, and move on—at least sometimes.

When I find myself feeling overwhelmed, I go back to the gratitude and compassion feelings and remind myself that I am fine regardless of what I complete. Then, I start breathing better and can think more clearly.

Then, I write down all my tasks and projections and look at my list. I get to decide what doesn't have to be done today, what is nice but not necessary. I use Stephen Covey's model of prioritization:[31] I create four categories: Important and urgent, important but not urgent, urgent but not important, and just not important. I also use a process from a book by David Allen, *Getting Things Done*[32]: I spend three hours every week reviewing everything from the previous week, including the mail, notes I've taken from meetings, my calendar, etc., and then I organize my ideals for the upcoming week. I highly recommend both systems.

When my list is complete, I look at what has to get done and decide how long each task will take by looking at how long I spent on similar tasks in the recent past. Still, I tend to underestimate how long things will take, so I try to add at least fifteen minutes to each task.

Next, I add my conditions of satisfaction. Monday's task is to organize for the week and plan out my highest priorities, my schedule, and what I need to give to my assistant. I won't answer the phone or deal with emails for at least two hours. This involves strategic thinking and planning instead of a lot of lower-level activities, such as responding to emails.

The hardest thing is to let go of something I feel *should* get done. Sometimes this is accepting that I haven't gotten to the mail and can let it go. The more I am in panic mode, the more likely I am to forget to do something that is important. The more compassionate I am with myself, the calmer I become and the more likely I am able to let go of the *shoulds*. Anytime I feel a *should* coming on, I stop and question it. Is this real—or is it based on some unrealistic perfectionist tendency such as, "I must clean off my desk."

Sometimes, I just need to let the articles I have read and want to file pile up and accept that it is not the best use of my time this week. And often, I can hire someone I can delegate lower-level tasks, too, so I can concentrate on harnessing my superpowers for my clients, my family, and myself.

The last step is to identify how I will acknowledge satisfaction. This is important even if I am really busy. Why? Because, once again, it's all about learning how to generate positive emotions so that I make decisions from a calm and confident place and not out of scarcity and fear. On Mondays, I tend to like to play a fun song on my iPod and dance or Hula-Hoop if possible—or at least listen to music that makes me smile. Then, after three minutes, I am ready for the next task.

Sometimes, I have to recalibrate when something doesn't quite work out or an unexpected situation arises, such as a client who needs a proposal as soon as possible. The foundation of making good decisions is to be disciplined about the acknowledgement that the positive emotions are critical to success—and *not* just a nice to-do if I have time. The more I take a pause, reflect on the situation, and find something positive, the easier I breathe and more productive I become. This takes practice. Let's build that resilience muscle.

Exercise #2: Determine your value

Every Monday, I evaluate the previous week in terms of reflecting on where I did or didn't add value. I learned this from Bob Dunham, who runs the Institute for Generative Leadership.[33] It has helped me realize how much value I'm adding and what types of situations trip me up. This has increased my self-confidence and belief in my wisdom.

Here's an example of the format and content I use for evaluating work tasks; you can make similar tables for other areas of your life, like family and fun. Feel free to use this or create your own.

Date/situation	Examples of where you've created value at work, the outcome, and why it was valuable	Examples of where you didn't create value, why not, the outcome, and what you learned
Team building	Participants valued gaining a clearer understanding of individual people on the team by using a personality assessment—helped to build stronger trust	Participants wanted to spend more time understanding their personality assessment results; I rushed through explaining the results. Next time participants want this, I need to go through each personality type one by one
Final coaching session	Client valued my direct observations and feedback	Wants even more direct feedback

Much to my surprise, this minuscule exercise was yielding big results. The first time I asked a high-potential leadership group to do the exercise, it was rated by several of the women in the group as one of the most valuable activities for that day. The second time I asked the women to do the exercise, many stated it was helping them to:

- Increase confidence, as they became aware they were constantly adding value

- Create a track record of successes

- Foster compassion, as they realized their successes outnumbered their mistakes

- Challenge their negative self-talk, which otherwise could overwhelm them, and instead force them to look at the facts

Give it a try for one month and see how you feel. What do you notice?

Now that we are working on building confidence, let's talk about ways to build resilience when slip-ups happen. The goal here is to work more effectively with others and feel more satisfied. Here are some questions to ask:

- What small steps can you take to start feeling like you're getting the most critical things done in the most efficient way?

- How can you ensure that others on your team, or your manager, are aligned on what success looks like?

- How can you manage your energy during and after a project's completion?

- What can you do to celebrate success?

Shackle-smashing actions

What is one small step you can take to break out of those shackles?

- Take five minutes to discuss any project given to you by your manager, colleague, or client. Ask questions such as: What is good enough? What does an excellent result look like? When do you really need this done? Then, make an agreement with everyone involved.

- Start keeping a success journal. Take five minutes every week to note something you did that went well or positive feedback you received. Feel free to spend more time as your successes increase.

- Identify tiny steps you can take on a big project, such as working for an hour and then taking a break; continue this pattern of working for an hour for three to five hours and give yourself a small reward after each hour, such as walking around the hall, getting a snack, or visiting a colleague.

- Identify a small way to celebrate satisfaction after you finish a goal at least two to three times a day; pick one, such as listening to music for two to three minutes.

What is one small physical action you can take to break out of those shackles?

Develop a physical satisfaction habit that helps you re-energize or recalibrate.

- This could include walking around the floor or outside or listening to music. My favorite is listening to a song that I can sing or makes me smile.

- Drop by someone's work area and thank the person for their contributions.

- When you start feeling overwhelmed or tight in your body, take five slow deep breaths from your stomach.

CHAPTER 7

Failure as a Badge of Honor

*"I really think a champion is defined
not by their wins but by how they
can recover when they fall."*

Serena Williams, after winning her
22nd Grand Slam title in tennis, July 2016

During one of the leadership development programs I facilitate, we brought in C-suite executives to share their wisdom with a group of high-potential women professionals. Joe, a panelist and CEO of a small financial services company, talked about failure. From his vantage point of the workplace for over forty years, he watched men view failure as a badge of honor. But women took each setback personally.

This idea of men viewing a setback as a badge triggered an A-ha moment for me. From my own experience and my work with hundreds of women professionals, I have observed that women tend to view their identity as tied to every win or loss. So, for women, a setback becomes a personal failure. What if we could learn from men and reframe how we think about setbacks?

Let me offer my story and a way of thinking about rebounding from losses that get us closer to the badge idea—and it involves baby steps.

My personal failure

My story begins with the Great Recession of 2009. As consulting and coaching assignments were drying up, I got offered an assignment to start up a leadership center in the microfinance industry. I knew nothing about microfinance, but I had just published my book about women and leadership and thought this would be a great opportunity to give back and help a much wider and global audience. Plus, I love a start-up.

My gut reaction when I interviewed with people who worked at this NGO (non-government organization) was that something didn't feel right. I did a little research and tried to learn something about the current leader and the organization but didn't find much. However, the team that I was to manage seemed terrific, and I knew I could hold any position for a year. I closed my business except for a few clients and began creating a new future.

Well, I found out it is not as easy as it looks to do anything for a year. After one year, I left the center due to major disagreements with the CEO. It was a painful loss, and it felt much more like a personal failure than a badge of honor.

I gave myself three months off to think about what I wanted to do next. My strategy for overcoming losses and disappointments is one I learned from a multitude of sources, including sports psychology, positive psychology, and ontological coaching.

Three actions to recover from a big slip-up

This approach is similar to the satisfaction, celebration, and recalibration habits described earlier, but it has a few minor differences— because it focuses on increasing the speed of recovery from a big slip-up. My own approach entails three sequential steps. Here's how I used them to rebound from my Great Recession Slip-up:

Be compassionate with yourself. This is first because it is hard to move on if you're beating yourself up. Write brief positive statements that can translate into visualizations or mantras that can create new possibilities. For example, I'd say to myself, "I trust the process of my life. The right opportunity will come to me. I trust myself to make smart decisions." I would say these affirmations to myself once a day as part of a ten- to fifteen-minute morning meditation for at least thirty days, so the way of thinking became a new habit and belief.

Reflect and focus on self-care. Give yourself time for self-reflection and self-care. Reflect and come to terms with what happened. I increased my phone calls with my executive coach from monthly to weekly to help me let go, figure out what was next, and move on. I also treated myself to regular massages, attended yoga classes, practiced daily meditation, and finally added acupuncture to the list, which really helped lift my spirits.

Reach out, but only to positive people. I was careful to only spend time with people who I knew understood me and stayed away from negative people. And, as I started to feel better, I reached out to former and current clients to talk with them once I had decided that I love being independent and wanted to rebuild an executive coaching and leadership development practice.

How the three-step resilience approach sped up my rebound from the Great Recession

What was interesting was how men and women reacted differently when I told them about my setback.

My first calls after I was fired were to two friends: one was a woman who invited me over to dinner to console me and the second was to another woman friend and her husband. It surprised me that while the woman was telling me that she was sorry it didn't work out, her husband kept saying, "Good riddance—that organization was a nightmare. Welcome back!" These two women friends' reactions were typical of what I felt. Women tended to focus on how I was feeling, whereas men viewed failure as not such a big deal.

One of my first client calls was to Pierre, a senior executive at a global financial services company. Pierre had been a consistent client over the last five years. He'd asked me to coach someone within his organization while I worked at the NGO. I called Pierre because he thought the microfinance experience was a good career move to broaden my international experience. When I told him that it didn't work out and I was coming back to coaching and consulting, he was thrilled. He said, "Good for you for taking the risk. I wish more of the guys who work for me would take a risk. Sorry it didn't work out. Welcome back. We will have more work for you. Just let me know what you are interested in doing."

After years of conditioning myself to avoid failure, I was amazed. As I continued to work with Pierre, I could feel that he saw me as more valuable than before I took this risk. I am now someone who is willing to fail. This was reinforced by another male friend, Gary, who said, "Remember, you do teach risk-taking—so now you have a story to tell!"

Jamie Dimon, CEO of JPMorgan Chase, once said that if you never take a risk, you've never really done anything interesting. My male friends helped me to realize Dimon was right. As I continue to coach both men and women, I realize how fearful most people are of failing.

My new strategy is to view setbacks more like the former competitive tennis player that I used to be: If I am not losing every so often, I am not stretching myself enough. I realized that I survived the setback and more importantly, I'm now viewing risk-taking as positive. I am well on my way towards viewing losing as a badge of honor. Game on.

Self-Compassion and Self-Esteem[34]

SELF-ESTEEM *"I am awesome"*	SELF-COMPASSION *"To err is human"*
Focus on building up and protecting self-image	Focus on improving or avoiding the mistake
Weaknesses are threats and create anxiety	Non-evaluation – kindness and acceptance
Evaluative – good or bad	New research suggests self-compassion leads to higher levels of well-being, optimism, and happiness and makes one more likely to achieve goals.
Some is useful for being courageous & influencing; does not predict greater success	

One of the fundamental components of building resilience is distinguishing self-compassion from self-esteem. Self-compassion—far from letting you off the hook—has been shown as critical and more important to success than self-esteem. Let's understand why.

Heidi Grant Halvorson, the associate director of the Motivation Science Center at Columbia Business School, found that when you are self-compassionate, you are not judging yourself harshly or becoming defensive. This lack of negative judgment and defensiveness engages you to feel higher levels of well-being, optimism, and happiness.

For example, her team asked participants in one study to take a self-compassionate or self-esteem view of a setback. The people who were taking the self-compassionate approach were told, "Imagine you are talking to yourself about this weakness from a compassionate and understanding perspective." In contrast, the people who were taking the self-esteem perspective were told, "Imagine you are talking to yourself about this weakness from a perspective of validating your positive qualities."

Who did better on the tests? Those students who viewed themselves from a self-compassionate perspective studied twenty-five percent longer and scored higher on a second test than participants who focused on bolstering their self-esteem.

It's important to note that Halvorson uses the less-common definition of self-esteem: less about respecting yourself for who you are, but more about self-praise—a somewhat narcissistic attempt to protect oneself from criticism. The more common definition is basically thinking well about yourself and recognizing that you're doing the best you can at this moment.

Why is self-compassion so powerful? It is non-judgmental and allows you to accept yourself and your shortcomings and be more positive. That, in turn, leads you to take more productive actions rather than feeling anxious or depressed because your self-esteem has been attacked.

We certainly need some self-esteem to apply for a stretch opportunity. But we also need self-compassion to bounce back more quickly and achieve life-long happiness and well-being. In today's fast-moving world, self-compassion is becoming your new BFF!

Shackle-smashing actions

Recovering from a big loss will take time. That means that you need to up the ante regarding self-care. You need to treat yourself with extreme gentleness and increase your self-care in a big way to help you recover faster.

What is one small action you can take to break out of those shackles?

- Become aware of how you talk to yourself. Now is the time for self-compassion. Listen and notice the thoughts and language you use. Start saying a simple mantra to yourself as often as needed—such as, "I made the best decision at the time with the information I had available to me. I have made it through difficult times before, and I will come through again."

- What are your favorite self-care activities? Getting a massage, taking long baths, visiting a nearby botanical garden, or spending time with good friends? Make sure to start doing at least one of these a week, along with a little something every day.

CHAPTER 8

Action 3: Getting Comfortable Being Uncomfortable

"In order to be irreplaceable one must always be different."

Coco Chanel, fashion designer, interview with
Michael Haedrich, *Coco Chanel: Her Life, Her Secrets*

Behavior that is socially acceptable for men often raises hostility or condescension when carried out by women. If a woman is very assertive one day and then gets upset the next day, people might label her "too emotional." With this smaller range of acceptable behavior, getting outside of your comfort zone can be riskier for women.

This explains the results of a 2015 survey by the Financial Women's Association (FWA), an organization for professional women who work in financial services, such as brokers, traders, salespeople, and human resources specialists. FWA asked members and women from the general public, "What are the most important things women can do to advance their careers in 2015?" The survey found that the number one reason women are not advancing in their careers is their unwillingness to go beyond their comfort zones. Seventy-eight percent of respondents recommended that women get out of their comfort zones to get promoted, fifty-nine percent said becoming more vocal/advocating for yourself, and forty-five percent suggested engaging in more networking.[35]

Why do women fail to get out of their comfort zones? According to the FWA study, it's that same old problem: women's perfectionist tendencies. As we've discussed, this perfectionist behavior can hold women back from speaking up at a meeting, applying for a new position, asking for a raise—unless they're absolutely sure they are right or will get what they are requesting.

What would make women less likely to share an unpopular view or ask for a raise?

Research from Sheryl Sandberg's book *Lean In* shows that women tend to be liked less as they become more senior—but men become more liked. When women step outside of the socially expected norms of being nice to assert themselves, they can be labeled bitches or "too aggressive." And it can be tough to shed those labels. Thus, risk-taking is riskier for women. So, it makes sense that women tend to be cautious; they understand they're treading on thin ice. Research shows that women typically only apply for a new job when they meet one hundred percent of the qualifications. Yet, men will apply when they can meet fifty percent or fewer. Because it seems riskier to contemplate failure, women want to make sure they will succeed.

What does this look like for women in the working world?

When I met Dina, a coaching client who is one of only a few women on a trading desk in a large global bank, she was beyond frustrated. A warm, gregarious person and a mother of two young children, she wanted to become a managing director but didn't feel like her boss was helping her get noticed or promoted. She noticed that the men were sending out congratulatory emails after she completed successful trades, using "I" and "We" language. Although this was outside of her comfort zone, she began to do it as well. Sometimes she gave herself credit and other times, she credited her male colleagues.

But she was told by senior leaders that she was too self-promotional. In contrast, her male colleague also sends out congratulatory emails on a regular basis using "I" and "We" language—but he is told he is on the path to success.

By the time Dina asked for an executive coach, she had almost given up on herself. When I asked Dina if she realized she was being viewed as self-promotional, she was surprised and hurt. She was just doing what most of her male colleagues did.

I'll share how Dina broke through these shackles in this chapter and the next, on building a safety net.

In today's fast-paced world, you must learn to get comfortable being uncomfortable. How can women do that in a safe and smart way, so they avoid the negative labels?

This chapter focuses on looking at how you approach risk-taking at work—and in life. You may find taking your chances at new options comes easily—or you might be a little more hesitant. We're all risk-takers, even if you would not describe yourself as one. Most of us have taken risks—gone to a new school, moved to a new state, started a new job, gone on a date, gotten married, had a baby, and so on. These risks are necessary for a happy and productive life. Risk-taking is a continuum. Some of us jump on as early adopters and others join the party later.[36] Once you understand yourself better, you'll be better able to safely start taking advantage of all those opportunities.

How to start getting comfortable being uncomfortable

About ten years ago, I first attended the Fear Workshop run by Mermer Blakeslee, the author of *A Conversation with Fear* and a highly accomplished thirty-year ski instructor.[37] I didn't start skiing until my twenties, and my goal as a skier was to advance beyond the intermediate doldrums. As a more conservative risk-taker, I tended to avoid steeper slopes until I was sure I could get safely down the hill without breaking a bone.

I signed up for Blakeslee's workshop because I wanted to gain more skills in tackling steep slopes so I could stop avoiding and start enjoying skiing intermediate and advanced intermediate slopes without freaking out. The women-only seminar ran for three days and included off-the-slope discussions and on-slope practice.

Blakeslee began the session by saying, "Fear is a critical component of an imaginative, creative, and interesting life."

I took in a big breath and realized she was right. Where would I—and most people—be if we didn't take risks? Just that realization was worth the cost of the workshop. Fear is my friend—even if she looks and feels a bit frightening at times. I want her in my life. I need to learn how to speak with her with kindness, not disdain.

This is where the self-compassion comes in. The challenge is the way our culture values positivity. No one wants to be Debbie Downer and express her fears or look weak. Blakeslee emphasized that it is alright to feel negative, that we were in a safe place. During the three days, Blakeslee explained that there are two types of risk-takers:

- Jane, who skis beautifully but doesn't want to tackle tough terrain unless she is pushed; she wants to make sure she can ski down the hill with skill and care.

- Fred, who likes to barrel down the hill regardless of his skill level.

Blakeslee described that these stereotypes are based on a couple she taught to ski. What isn't surprising is that Jane seems stereotypically female and Fred, male. I can see myself in Jane as I analyze the risk in advance and want to make sure I will be successful.

During the three-day workshop, we learned several skiing techniques to help us navigate more challenging terrain. As I faced my yikes zone going down a narrow steep trail, I hit ice and slid down the trail until I faced a tree. As I began to panic and attempted to sit down on my skis, hoping that I could get closer to the ground, my instructor gently told me to breathe and just take one turn at a time. Gradually and slowly, I made one big turn as instructed. I was facing my fear one turn at a time. This was a key technique we learned in the seminar: Narrow the focus, and lower the task. The instructor was taking me away from staring at the nearby trees and rocks and the steepness of the mountain.

Upon returning to the bottom of the hill and looking up at what I had just conquered, I realized my comfort zone had been expanded. I felt empowered to approach steeper slopes—because I now had a strategy for making it safe.

What is a smart risk? How do you make it safe?

Risk involves taking actions that could result in a negative impact. Taking risks is smart because it could move you towards your goals and career success.

Examples of risk at work include sharing an unpopular view at a meeting, raising your hand for a new assignment, or engaging in a new activity, such as networking or delegating.

Making it safe involves actions designed to protect yourself or your team from harm. Examples include being self-compassionate, building a strategic network, working with your approach to risk-taking, asking for support, or being politically savvy.

Two steps to taking a smart risk:
Recognizing your approach to risk-taking, identifying ways to leverage your strengths, and seizing opportunities for growth.

Identifying, and then expanding, your comfort zone. Develop a strategy and steps to continually expand that comfort zone; make it safe to stretch and grow.

Background on risk-taking mindsets

There are different ways that people think about risk-taking. Dr. Roger Birkman enlisted in the US Army Air Corps and became a B-17 bomber pilot during World War II. He became interested in the exploration of individual psychological differences.

Dr. Birkman noticed that even though the pilots received the same training, they managed stress differently. Some pilots seemed to thrive when thrown into difficult situations, while others did not. The first iteration of the assessment was developed in 1951, and the version as we know it today was developed in the 1960s.

The Birkman Method® is designed to provide insight into what specifically drives a person's behavior, with the goal of creating greater choice and more self-responsibility. It is empirically supported by numerous reliability and validity studies. If you want to learn more or take the instrument, go to birkman.com/about-birkman/our-story-growth.

The Birkman instrument inspired me to develop two risk-taking mindsets.

Two mindsets—Driven to Prove and Driven to Succeed

The risk-taking mindset is inspired by Challenge, one of the components of the Birkman instrument that measures the mental dialogue (or self-talk) that is behind behavior. Challenge is measuring something that is invisible and makes it visible. We can see the behavior, but we often don't understand the mental messages that are translated into actions. It is those internal messages around what defines success and self-worth that Challenge describes. This includes how people think about risk-taking with some people only wanting to engage in activities that leverage their strengths whereas others would rather try something new.

I have worked with Doug Leonard, an expert in The Birkman Method, to identify two mindsets around what drives and motivates people. Most professional women typically embody one or the other, though a rare few function well with a foot in each camp.

Driven to Prove: You have a high need to prove yourself and take on new challenges; your Challenge score is high. Those who are driven to prove are less focused on their image externally, yet they validate themselves externally by what gets done. The usual behavior of a Driven to Prove individual is to be seduced by complex challenging problems and stretch goals—the harder the better. Strong-willed, determined, aware of personal shortcomings, they accept greater risks—regardless of expertise—as a way to prove themselves. They need to work with continually elevated goals as an opportunity to demonstrate to themselves that they can handle challenges.

Driven to Succeed: You have a high need for self-protection and for showing how you excel in your core competencies but find new challenges that are outside your core strengths threatening or uncomfortable; thus, you have a low Challenge score. People who are Driven to Succeed act to protect a naturally existing positive sense of self-worth. They are typically confident of their abilities, pleasant, persuasive. They take calculated risks based upon personal expertise. They work toward achievable goals where they can shine and receive praise/recognition to create an image of success.

Essentially, low risk tolerance translates to Driven to Succeed; high risk tolerance, Driven to Prove.

One of the common denominators of Driven to Prove and Driven to Succeed individuals is that their identity is linked to behavior. Whether high or low—what we do is driven by how we create a sense of worth for ourselves. It is a continuum of mindset around risk-taking. Driven to Prove and Driven to Succeed are complementary. They share a common intensity to succeed. Each perspective offers benefits—and challenges.

How each manages stress

When things go wrong, these divergent viewpoints can lead to intense friction. No one wants to give up their perspective because it's strongly linked to our identity. How you feel good about yourself is in jeopardy and is being compromised.

Under pressure, a Driven to Prove becomes extremely critical and demanding of herself and others. She feels inadequate but is reluctant to accept success without critical review.

A Driven to Succeed under pressure tends to blame personal problems or shortcomings on situational external factors, protecting the self, and doesn't like public recognition of a problem.

As mentioned, there's a third type of risk-taker besides Driven to Succeed and Driven to Prove: Someone who can see both sides and respond situationally.

Determine *your* approach to risk-taking

Review the following chart and take the self-assessment to determine where you are on the continuum of risk-taking. I'll share several examples in each category: famous people as well as my own coaching clients.

We all have various perceptions of risk and of ourselves, so don't be surprised if you change your perception. It's common to start out thinking you're Driven to Succeed only to discover you're actually closer to the middle of the continuum. There's a common bias in many organizations that Driven to Prove seems more attractive and that Driven to Succeed seems kind of wimpy. Remember, people with both mindsets are risk-takers; they just approach risk differently. And, if all else fails, ask a relative or friend who knows you well. Your mother or spouse will usually know.

DRIVEN TO SUCCEED	SEES BOTH SIDES	DRIVEN TO PROVE
• Analyses risk in advance		• Analyses the risk after the fact
• Stretches core strengths		• Focuses on potential
• Sets goals that are attainable		• Seeks elevated goals and focuses on proving the self
• Goes step-by-step to ensure success		• Under stress – becomes critical of self and others and beats self up, even in public.
• Under stress – shows a positive image to the world and blames shortcomings on external factors		

Taking the self-assessment

Take a moment and reflect about how you think and act regarding risk-taking—both at work and in life.

This assessment is designed to help you understand how you naturally expand your comfort zone and take risks. Everyone is a risk-taker, and this self-assessment will illuminate your preferences.

Answer the questions quickly, spending no more than a second or two on each.

Rate yourself honestly on a 1–10 scale. It doesn't matter where you are on the scale. The goal is to provide you with increased self-awareness about your risk-taking mindset and tendencies so that you can increase your options. All approaches can be successful. Complete and determine your approach.

Reflection	Scale		Your Score
When you are considering taking a risk, how do you tend to mitigate the risk?	(1) You prefer to evaluate your ability to do it in advance of committing, to set yourself up to succeed; the goal is to protect your positive sense of self	→ (10) You prefer to commit first and then figure out how you will accomplish what you've committed to. You are driven to prove yourself through accomplishments	
When you're seeking out a new opportunity, do you tend to focus more on setting attainable goals or on proving yourself?	(1) You want to build upon your core strengths and set attainable goals, such as becoming an accounting partner	→ (10) You are energized by setting elevated goals that stretch you beyond your current skill level, such as an accountant with a creative flair starting a business as an interior decorator	
How do you approach attaining your goals?	(1) You assume that you need to go step-by-step, progressing from easy to more difficult steps to ensure success	→ (10) You tend to experiment and try things out as opportunities present themselves.	
Where do you derive the most satisfaction when taking risks?	(1) You enjoy achieving goals that harness your core strengths and let you work in a success-oriented environment	→ (10) You enjoy the challenge of proving to yourself that you can do something you didn't think you could	
How often do you ask for a push and/or constructive/ positive feedback from key stakeholders and your support team?	(1) You reflect privately— but when you solicit others' opinions, you seek out reinforcement and positive feedback	→ (10) You regularly ask for—and act on—constructive feedback	

Reflection	Scale		Your Score
What sorts of goals do you set in your personal life and in your work life?	(1) You tend to focus on mastering a few things before sharing them publicly	(10) You tend to seek out challenges in all areas of your life; you could be going to school at night, learning photography for fun, running in your first marathon, and seeking leadership roles at work	
When you experience the stress of risk-taking, how do you show it?	(1) You tend to show a positive image to the world and focus on what's going right; you're uncomfortable with public recognition of a problem	(10) You tend to beat yourself up even in public and can be hard on yourself; you keep pushing yourself to achieve your potential in all areas of your life	
		Total:	

Scoring

7–35: You tend toward Driven to Succeed. You tend to feel most comfortable analyzing the risk in advance, focusing on stretching your core strengths, and setting goals that are attainable. You go step-by-step to ensure success and tend to show a positive image to the world.

35–50: You're comfortable going back and forth between Driven to Succeed and Driven to Prove. Sometimes you may jump right into something, and other times you may plan it out. You understand both approaches and consciously and comfortably go back and forth, depending on the situation.

50–70: You're most comfortable with a Driven to Prove approach. You tend to analyze the risk after the fact, focus on your potential, seek elevated goals, and focus on proving yourself. You tend to be hard on yourself and enjoy the challenge of jumping into new opportunities.

Understanding your results

Many times, those of you whose scores are in the middle might feel uncertain about your preferences. This is normal. Three approaches can help you understand your tendencies:

- Listen to your gut instinct as to what feels most comfortable.

- Ask someone who has known you for a long time.

- Review some examples of well-known and real people.

Examples of well-known leaders

Here are my assessments of some well-known people. What do you think?

Driven to Prove: Mark Zuckerberg, founder of Facebook and its parent company, Meta Platforms, and Vera Wang, CEO of her own clothing company. Mark started a new venture with no previous leadership experience, and Vera went from being the youngest fashion editor of *Vogue* magazine at age twenty-three right out of college to starting her own company, making wedding dresses seventeen years later because she was frustrated with the slim selection of dresses available. Vera was an art history major at Sarah Lawrence College with no education in the clothing business.[38]

Driven to Succeed: Jeff Immelt, former CEO of General Electric (GE), and Mary Barra, the CEO of General Motors (GM). Both had long careers with these companies and rose through the ranks. For example, Mary Barra attended the GM Institute—now called

Kettering University—as an undergrad and earned a bachelor's in electrical engineering. She started working at GM as a co-op student during college to help pay off her tuition and took various jobs and moved up the ranks.[39]

My approach to risk: Driven to Succeed (and yes, we do take risks)!

I identify as more of a Driven to Succeed. The core strength that I have built my career around is coaching competitive people to play their best game. I began my career as a competitive tennis player and junior tennis champion, became a tennis coach, obtained a master's degree in psychology, became a therapist, and worked in a school and government agency, changed careers to training and development in business, started my own executive coaching and training company, and began writing self-help books for women to overcome their perfectionist tendencies.

The scariest risk for me was to leave a high-paying job to start my own company. But I was willing to do it because I had analyzed the risk in advance, saved money, and sought out entrepreneur coaching to help me succeed.

As I've gotten older, I've moved towards Driven to Prove. That's how I started my new career of writing self-help books. Granted, these books are based on topics in which I am an expert. Once again, I approach it step-by-step, taking a writing class and hiring a coach to help me navigate the publishing world.

At the same time, my Driven to Succeed mindset is ever-present.

I'm now exploring writing a memoir about my relationship with my developmentally disabled brother, Chris. I'm passionate about this because, after my parents passed away five years ago, I became an advocate for expanding my brother's ability to assert himself and take charge of his life. The surprising part of advocating for Chris is that he is teaching me a lot about myself and my perfectionism. Chris is making progress, albeit very slowly.

Chris is also reminding me—someone who does coaching for a living—to focus on progress and small changes versus comparing one's results to an unrealistic standard of success. Chris is teaching me to stay present and curious, and I continue to invest in having joyful experiences with Chris, I know he will continue to take tiny steps forward. And that is good enough.

After supporting and witnessing Chris's growth using my coaching skills, I believe that others might benefit from the lessons I learned, the ways I failed, the ways I succeeded, both for those with developmentally disabled relatives and fellow perfectionists.

But I have limited experience with disabled people and have never written a memoir. So I signed up for a memoir writing workshop, in which I received a lot of support around the memoir focused on my brother. And I now have a book outline.

Writing this book continues to expand my comfort zone and reminds me of the importance of continuing to stretch. As we get older, unless we take active steps, our comfort zone shrinks. But if you stretch it on a regular basis, it actually gently enlarges. I have no idea where this new book idea will take my life, but I'm open to the possibilities.

Why stretching outside of your comfort zone is so important for everyone

When I lead a training, I openly share that I am a perfectionist-in-recovery who hates to do anything we are not going to win or do well. When I told the story about playing in my first tennis tournament in twenty years, a participant named Sheryl had an A-ha moment.

Sheryl smiled as she listened to my story. She was in her late fifties and all her children, husband, and friends played tennis. They often asked her to play. But she usually declined because she said she wasn't good enough. The light bulb had gone off, and she began to entertain thoughts of playing tennis again.

After Sheryl shared her story, several other women told similar stories of how they were too afraid of doing something poorly and turned down opportunities.

Tiffany, who had just become engaged, said her fiancé wanted her to enter a sporting event to raise money for charity. Tiffany went home after the first day of the seminar and told her fiancé that she wanted to do the event with him. He was shocked; he hadn't thought she would be up for such a frivolous activity.

Why does this matter?

It might not seem like a big deal to not play a silly little tennis tournament. But every time you think, "Oh, I can't do that," your comfort zone begins to shrink. It shrinks and shrinks until you find yourself only taking very small and calculated risks. You wake up, and suddenly you're much older—and very afraid. As Sheryl realized in the seminar, she was in her late fifties, bored in her job, and not having much fun outside of work either.

In contrast, you can become wiser by learning from all those lessons learned over the years. But you're going to have to fight this shrinking comfort zone.

I am in my fifties and having the time of my life now. I'm taking more smart risks than ever before. I continuously push myself out of my comfort zone in small ways, such as playing in a minor tennis tournament, participating in a memoir writing workshop, and taking on clients in a new industry.

The A-ha for me as I listened to Sheryl and the others in the workshop was that people need to see that these small examples in their personal lives can help them in business. Sheryl felt stuck in business, and she was also limiting herself in her personal life. Start taking risks where it is easier and safer. You can reverse the shrinkage of your comfort zone one small step at a time.

Think of a time you took a risk and succeeded. Write this down. Share it with a friend. Ask your friend what type of risk-taker she/he/they thinks you are.

Two examples of successful leaders

Two women that I've coached embody the two mindsets. In the following summaries, I've kept most of the crucial details without giving away their identities. Review their characteristics, careers, and lives. As you read their stories, ask yourself: What motivates them? How do they deal with stress?

Listen and see to whom you most relate.

Driven to Prove

I met Carol at a women's business networking event. She was eager to hire me as a coach and decided to do so on her own, without company support. Raised in a small town in Florida, she'd had several careers. She'd owned an exercise studio and had worked in a small family business.

After doing several smaller projects for the business, she was relocated to New York City by a real estate company to be the accountant/controller for one of the biggest real estate developments and had been living in the Big Apple for about five years. She was excited to be part of a new opportunity; she enjoyed being a part of start-ups, creative projects, and loved teamwork.

In our work together, she welcomed tough feedback. She was eager to face the positive and constructive and wanted to know what she could do to rise up in a very male-dominated and tough industry.

Carol was always doing many things at the same time. I would get exhausted just listening to her life. When she wasn't working sixty- to eighty-hour weeks, she was taking up Feng Shui, photography, French, or babysitting her relatives' dogs. She also loved organizing parties. She loved living in the city for all the challenges and possibilities it had to offer.

Driven to Succeed

Bethany came to me through a company-sponsored coaching program. She was ambitious and wanted to become a managing director. From the Northeast, she had moved to California to join her husband. Working in an investment bank's technology group since college, she really enjoyed being well-liked by her team, mentoring junior bankers, and winning new business. She wanted to grow her skills by learning more about financing, expanding her network, and becoming more organizationally savvy. She believed she'd find success by becoming an expert in understanding the technology space and being viewed as a leader by the junior- and senior-level bankers.

Outside of work, she had just had a new baby and would enjoy downtime at home, watching football games with her husband.

DRIVEN TO PROVE	DRIVEN TO SUCCEED
Carol: CPA and VP controller for large real estate developer	*Bethany: Director at top global investment bank, graduated top of Ivy league school*
• Driven to Prove	• Driven to Succeed
• Came from small town. College graduate in a family business, she was recruited to move to NYC	• Came from the Northeast and moved to CA to be with husband; in same product group and firm since college
• Enjoys start-ups, complex projects, creativity, and teamwork	• Enjoys being well-liked, being asked for her opinion, mentoring, and winning mandates
• Wants to work in an environment that challenges her; seeks opportunities to do new projects and continue her education	• Prefers an environment in which she can succeed without huge risks and has strong credibility and people who support her
• Energized by achieving goals, being included in key start-up projects, getting her master's degree, learning French, photography, and Feng Shui	• Energized by becoming a managing director, maintaining and expanding client relationships, expanding her network, and learning more about financing
• Sets continued elevated goals	• Sets escalating but attainable goals
• Seeks honest feedback from people she trusts	• Seeks reinforcement and positive feedback
• Finds challenges emerge as she takes advantage of new opportunities and proves herself	• Finds challenges by stretching her core strengths
• Seeks an environment that offers a lot of personal challenges	• Creates a success-oriented environment

How to expand your comfort zone

Now you know what type of risk-taker you are. The goal is to understand what your comfort zone looks like and what your safety needs are so that you can safely stretch without a fight-or-flight response. What you don't want is to take a risk, freak out, and then vow never to take a risk again. This section has two parts: understanding the four zones—and where you tend to live more of your life, and understanding how you think about making things SAFE and learning ways to make risk-taking more sustainable and comfortable.

Let's define the four zones and look at how much time you spend in these zones

Four performance zones:

- **Blah Zone:** Area where you feel bored and lack interest or desire.

- **Comfort Zone:** Area where you feel at ease without any challenge.

- **Stretch Zone:** Trying out new behaviors that energize you and allow you to grow without causing a breakdown response or a significant diminishing in effectiveness.

- **Yikes Zone:** Attempting new behaviors that are so threatening to your self-esteem or sense of well-being that they provoke a flight-or-fight response.

The specifics are different for everyone; an activity in your Comfort Zone might be in my Yikes Zone. Here are examples:

- **Blah Zone:** Watching TV, playing video games, taking a nap.

- **Comfort Zone:** Analyzing a spreadsheet, delivering a training program you've done numerous times, traveling to a city you have visited extensively, or doing any kind of activity that is very familiar.

- **Stretch Zone:** Presenting your analysis to senior leaders, delivering a new training program, traveling to a city in a foreign country that you have never visited, asking for and/ or engaging in a new and unfamiliar task.

- **Yikes Zone:** Speaking in front of an enormous audience in which you are completely unfamiliar, engaging in an activity that feels threatening to your well-being such as skiing down a double black diamond slope, traveling alone to a city where you can't read the signs or understand the language.

How to expand your Comfort Zone?

You will expand your Comfort Zone differently depending on what type of risk-taker you are. The first step is to become aware of how much time you spend in these zones. If you're a Driven to Prove, you may live mostly in a Stretch Zone and dip frequently into the Yikes Zone; the Driven to Succeed may live mostly in the Comfort Zone, with a tiny amount in Stretch and a little in Blah.

If you are Driven to Succeed, consider gradually increasing time spent in the Stretch Zone. In contrast, the Driven to Prove person might want to spend a little less time in the Stretch or Yikes Zones and spend some time in the Comfort or Blah Zones to reflect and recover. There is no right or wrong approach. Success in expanding your Comfort Zone is gradually expanding your ability to take smart risks without burning out.

Let's examine a couple of examples of how a Driven to Prove and Driven to Succeed manage their Comfort Zones and reflect on which zone you tend to live in and one small change you might want to consider to be more productive.

How each mindset manages the stress of risk-taking

Here are the challenges each mindset faces when attempting risks—simple things to be aware of and to manage the stress of taking risks. If you are not sure which mindset is most like you, usually the description of how they manage stress tells the story.

DRIVEN TO PROVE— CAROL	DRIVEN TO SUCCEED— BETHANY
• Internalizes stress—but she is comfortable beating herself up in public, "really screwed this up"	• Uncomfortable with public recognition of a problem
• Focuses on potential	• Tends to blame the problem on the situation
• Can be hard on herself—has to monitor self-talk	• Focuses on what is going right
• Can spend too much time in Yikes and Stretch Zones—leading to burnout	• Focuses on one thing at a time
	• Can spend too much time in the Comfort Zone, which can lead to procrastination or avoidance

Here are two stories illustrating how Carol and Bethany managed their Comfort Zones during stressful times.

I worked with both Carol and Bethany during the Great Recession. Carol, who worked in real estate development, was miserable because all her projects were stalled. So, she started spending more time on photography and Feng Shui and adopted another dog.

Much to Carol's surprise, she got laid off. Carol had ignored the signals around her, including layoffs and the jockeying to hold onto fewer leadership roles. In contrast, Bethany said everything was going great because she had a job and many of her colleagues were losing theirs, yet she nonetheless spent time looking for a new job.

When Carol was laid off, she learned that she needed to spend more time reflecting in the Blah and Comfort Zones versus spending too much time in the Stretch and Yikes Zones when things were not going well. Carol took some time off and evaluated her next risk in advance. In contrast, once Bethany realized the company was hemorrhaging, she pushed herself to spend more time in the Stretch Zone; although she didn't enjoy it, she spent more time networking, because she knew it was critical to her future success.

Bethany ended up in a better place more quickly than Carol because she stretched outside of her Comfort Zone. The foundation of managing risk is understanding what you look like under stress and developing habits that allow you to continue grow.

Exercise to expand your Comfort Zone

Estimate the percentage of time you spend in each zone in a typical week. For example, my week might look like this:

Zone	Percentage of Time
Blah	10%
Comfort	50%
Stretch	30%
Yikes	10%

Then, ask yourself if this allocation encourages the changes you want to make. Are you too comfortable, or too burned out? I don't want to get too comfortable and fight against that.

What single small shift could you make to help you expand your comfort zone? For example, I would like to spend a little more time in the Stretch Zone. This could involve me playing tennis against someone who is better than me, pitching business to one more person a week, or asking a client or friend for feedback.

What does your typical week look like?

Zone	Percentage of Time
Blah	
Comfort	
Stretch	
Yikes	

Let's look at how you stretch your Comfort Zone. What do you do to make it safe?

How do you stretch? Think about a time in your personal or professional life where you learned something new, and you enjoyed the process.

For example, as a Driven to Succeed person, I seek out coaches and take a step-by-step approach. I learned how to deliver presentations by joining Toastmasters and practicing in front of a safe audience, then gradually started presenting to small and eventually to larger groups. I also hired a presentation coach to watch me and offer feedback.

The starting point is understanding your approach to risk-taking and what your Comfort Zone looks like. Everyone has a different Comfort Zone. For the Driven to Prove, stretching might mean jumping in and doing something new, then reflecting in the Comfort Zone to determine what's working.

Describe a time when you took a risk that you enjoyed taking.

Learning to make it safe

People who are Driven to Succeed or Driven to Prove have different definitions of safety. Successful risk-taking involves knowing what safety means to you. Here's a Making-it-Safe exercise.

Creating your safety checklist

Draft your safety checklist. Review the list, whether you are Driven to Prove or Driven to Succeed.

Identify the areas where you tend to do well—and at least one new habit that you want to add or commit to doing more regularly to make risk-taking safer.

Review your example of the risk you took that you enjoyed. What safety habits did you use? Answer these questions:

- What safety habits do you use most frequently?

- What one or two safety habits that you don't currently practice would you like to add to your repertoire?

- How would this benefit you and link to your long- and short-term goals? In other words, for the sake of what?

- What's one small step that you could take to build that muscle?

As an example, this was my approach when I was seeking a career change:

What safety habits do you use most frequently? "I built a network and found a couple of mentors."

What one or two safety habits that you don't currently practice would you like to add to your repertoire? "I realize that I don't receive that much honest feedback. I don't seek it out often enough."

How would this benefit you and link to your larger and short-term goals? Or, for the sake of what? "When I started asking for more honest feedback, my boss suggested I take a coaching skills course, as he thought this would be a great next step for me in my career."

What's one small step you could take to build that muscle? I looked at how I could build on my strengths. "I could reach out monthly and ask for honest feedback on my business plan, my training approach, my speeches, and so on."

How to expand your Comfort Zone and build resilience

Here is a list of actions designed to keep you mentally and physically buoyant and increase the speed of rebounding from slip-ups. Review and identify which actions you've already taken and which you might be willing to experiment with. Then identify one or two small steps that you can add to your repertoire. Select one that seems the easiest to add to your day-to-day life. Practicing even one of these actions on a regular basis could enhance your comfort with risk-taking.

	How often have you taken these actions? 1 (never) to 5 (sometimes) to 10 (always)	How likely are you to do this? 1 (never) to 5 (sometimes) to 10 (always)	Select one that seems easiest to add to your day-to-day life
Find 10 things to feel grateful for every day			
Have compassion for yourself—give yourself a break, especially when you slip up			
Set clear boundaries; ask yourself: Is this mine to fix?			
Identify what satisfaction will look like to you and/or key stakeholders?			
Determine if you need to put out 100% to get this done, or will 75% be good enough?			
Regularly take time to identify/reflect on achievements			
Celebrate satisfaction when you have taken risks (whether or not you succeeded)			

	How often have you taken these actions? 1 (never) to 5 (sometimes) to 10 (always)	How likely are you to do this? 1 (never) to 5 (sometimes) to 10 (always)	Select one that seems easiest to add to your day-to-day life
Carefully study your failures so you understand how to do better the next time. Identify generally positive qualities about yourself and specific actions that contributed to the slip-up. Strategize about how you can remedy them in the future.			
Build and maintain relationships with 10–15 key stakeholders and supporters			
Periodically seek out honest feedback/advice/counsel from diverse sources			
Reach out first to someone you trust before trying to gain wider buy-in for a new idea or initiative			
Do a power pose for two minutes before taking part in Stretch Zone activities			

Exercise: Making it safe

After you've reviewed your results from the safety checklist and the Driven to Prove/Driven to Succeed lists, identify a habit that you want to build upon or add to your repertoire.

How Driven to Prove and Driven to Succeed types make it safe

Now that you are self-aware of your safety habits, review the following list to see which safety habits tend to be more natural for you and which you may need to add to your repertoire.

Driven to Prove

- Needs partners/coaches to rein her in, help her focus, be supportive.

- Calculates risks in advance before overcommitting.

- Has to learn to lighten up and accept and give praise without critique.

- Needs to be realistic about performance standards.

- Needs to spend some time in Comfort or Blah Zones.

Driven to Succeed

- Needs partners/coaches to give her a push and provide honest feedback/support.

- Must avoid taking the easy way out; instead, continuously look for ways to improve.

- Has to learn to accept feedback without excuses and analyze it carefully.

- Will benefit by taking more uncalculated personal risks.

- Needs to not trap herself in the Comfort or Blah Zones.

What happened to Dina and wrap-up

Returning to Dina, she began to understand that she tends toward Driven to Succeed. Her first brave step was that she asked for an executive coach. At her organization, this was not commonplace—though she knew men who had asked for a coach and found it helpful. In turn, her coach provided the gentle—and sometimes not-so-gentle—push that Dina needed to start having different types of conversations and not just sending out self-congratulatory emails out of frustration.

She realized that when she was more inclusive in both reaching out beforehand and giving more people credit along with herself, she was perceived as a stronger team player, which enabled her to be viewed more positively. In the next chapter, we'll explore how Dina built a safety net of key allies—and how crucial this was to her success.

Now that you have a greater awareness of how you think about risk-taking, this will lead you to expand your Comfort Zone more often—because you have a strategy. Once I learned that I can do anything as long as I do it in a step-by-step way, my Comfort Zone continued to expand. That's what we are going for—a more expansive, productive, and joyful life.

Shackle-smashing actions

You want to feel more confident and comfortable stretching outside of your Comfort Zone so you're ready to take more small risks. You want to learn the best approach for expanding your options, so you make risk-taking a habit. Then, stretching becomes the new normal. Remember, no small step is too small.

What's one new safety habit that you will commit to practicing regularly?

Driven to succeed examples:

- As a Driven to Succeed, a small step I take is talking compassionately to myself when I feel disappointed after I didn't win a new piece of business. And every month, I discuss my experiences with my business coach, asking for career guidance.

- Driven to Succeeds benefit from making sure there are rewards both small and large, such as listening to music, taking a walk, or getting a coffee. Recently, I bought myself a new pair of earrings after having the courage to conduct a very challenging conversation.

- As a Driven to Succeed, I spend two minutes Power Posing in the ladies' room or a private office before a challenging event. This physical movement helps to calm me down.

Driven to prove examples:

- Carol, my Driven to Prove client from the earlier example, hired me as a coach to help her navigate her career so she would make more thoughtful career choices. Our work together involved providing her with honest feedback after watching her give a presentation and discussing risks that might not be working out quite as planned.

- Driven to Proves benefit from activities, like taking five minutes to reflect and write or call a friend and share, especially after experiencing a challenging day, making a mistake, or acting outside their Comfort Zone (regardless of the outcome). The tricky part for Driven to Proves is that they aim high. One of my clients gives herself a thirty-minute drop-by at a coffee house to read fiction.

CHAPTER 9

Action 4: Creating a Safety Net of Trusted Relationships

"Sometimes high-potential women have a difficult time asking for help because they don't want to appear stumped. Being unsure about how to proceed is the most natural feeling in the world. I feel that way all the time. Asking for input is NOT a sign of weakness but often the first step to finding a path forward."

— Sheryl Sandberg[40]

The better your network of trusted advisors, the more freedom you have to be yourself, take risks, and fail/rebound without negative consequences. For example, if Dina had had a trusted relationship with someone in a powerful position, that person could have disputed the claim that she was too self-promotional.

Dina realized that since she wasn't getting the support she needed from her manager, she needed to expand her network and find it elsewhere. Dina had many encouraging colleagues; she just had to learn how to ask for their support. But many women, especially high-potential women, are reluctant to ask for that help.

In this chapter, you'll see how Dina and other women have broken out of their shackles by realizing that Sheryl Sandberg is right: Asking for help can be the first step forward. We will provide simple tools and many examples of how women have learned how to ask for help in a smart way.

Here's a step-by-step approach to creating a supportive community:

- Build someone's emotional bank account, which is a metaphor for the amount of trust in the relationship. For example, when you ask a new co-worker to articulate the best way to communicate with them—email, text, or some other method—that is a small gesture that makes a deposit in someone's emotional bank account. We will discuss this later on.

- Make requests.

- Ask for feedback.

- Create a more strategic network. This means you are forming relationships with people who can provide both long-term guidance and support as well as assistance with day-to-day challenges. We will define this and offer ways to do this.

Why building trust can be challenging for perfectionist women

Until I was thirteen years old, I got only As in math. But I struggled with geometry. My math teacher at the time told me that I was not good at math, so I gave up.

Sadly, my story is not uncommon. As we discussed earlier, Carol Dweck, in her book, *Mindset,* says that women trust other people's opinions of themselves too much. Why? Dweck says that little girls often appear perfect growing up. They are well-behaved, cute, and helpful—and everyone tells them so. Girls learn to trust people's estimates of them so much that if people criticize them, they think it must be true.[41]

In contrast, Dweck's research has found that boys get eight times more criticism for their conduct than girls. Boys are constantly being disparaged. Having grown up playing tennis with a lot of boys, I noticed they seemed to enjoy calling each other names such as slow, lazy, or moron. Because being insulted is part of the experience of growing up male in our culture, Dweck says males think twice before deciding if someone's criticism is worth believing. But because girls grow up being praised, and only later does that praise turn to criticism, she found that even at the top universities in the United States, women say that other people's opinions are a good barometer. She says that fields such as math and science need to be made more hospitable to women if they are to succeed.

Thus, we perfectionists set ourselves up to fail—because, to avoid external criticism, our self-esteem requires demonstrating that we can do everything. We never want to look weak. But the problem is even worse because most of us are not comfortable bragging about our accomplishments; we believe the work should speak for itself. Like many other women on trading floors I've worked with, Dina chose not to ask anyone for feedback. Unfortunately, hard work is not enough. Research shows that you need a sponsor to advocate for your promotion and that those with sponsors are more likely to receive promotions.[42]

How to easily build the safety net

For most of us perfectionists, this is going to involve getting out of your comfort zone. I have narrowed it down to three simple steps:

- **Identify what trust means to you.** Take simple steps to be selectively vulnerable so you can build that trust without damaging your reputation.

- **Take three small actions that will build trust more quickly.** Make deposits in people's emotional bank accounts, make requests, and ask for feedback.

- **Build a strategic network.** Make sure you have enough diversity—around ten to fifteen people with whom you have varied levels of trust—so you are not just asking your friends for advice.

Defining trust

Trust is the foundation for the most efficient and productive relationships. When you work with people you trust, you accomplish tasks with more ease and speed. You don't have to spend time agonizing over long emails or proposals explaining your position. You can share your view in a straightforward manner—and people are more apt to go along.

Trust means different things to different people. You know you have a supportive network of trusted advisors if you have:

- People who give you useful, honest feedback, so you have fewer surprises.

- One key person within your organization who helps you navigate the politics.

- People who give you the benefit of the doubt.

- People who offer to help you.

- People who share more critical information about changes in the business or leadership.

- People who invite you to meetings.

- People who offer compliments.

- People from whom you can ask a favor.

- People who are more open to your ideas/requests.

How do you gain these benefits?

Everyone wants to experience these relationships at work. As we all know, it takes time and involvement with others to build that trust. The premise of this book is that small actions can lead to big results. Creating trusted relationships is no different. It involves small moments of being selectively vulnerable.

Vulnerability

SELECTIVE VULNERABILITY	UNSAFE VULNERABILITY
You are discerning about whom you open yourself up to. You may choose to be vulnerable—BUT not at your own expense	Letting it all hang out.
• Presenting a warm physical presence • Smiling • Listening first	Hugging everyone, crying in front of everyone/anytime

SELECTIVE VULNERABILITY	UNSAFE VULNERABILITY
• Asking for help or feedback • Sharing an unpopular opinion or interests that are important to you • Apologizing sincerely when you have made a mistake and taking corrective action	Using vulnerability to deal with unmet needs, get attention, or engage in shock/awe behaviors

As you can see from the chart, selective vulnerability is not about self-disclosure. It's about thoughtfully finding ways to connect with others, be productive, and get results in a way that does not compromise your reputation. As someone who grew up as a perfectionist and a competitive athlete, I viewed vulnerability as the enemy. My new view of vulnerability came about from reading and listening to the work of Brené Brown. A research professor at the University of Houston, her many books include, *Daring Greatly: How the Courage to Be Vulnerable Transforms the Way We Live, Love, Parent, and Lead.*[43]

Most of the women I coach never want to be vulnerable. One client, Sabrina, would always go out of her way to make eye contact with the president of her division when he would walk by her desk on the trading floor. Sabrina was a trader who was a strong producer, but not very well-known. A huge small step was for Sabrina to smile and say hello to the president. Then, she gradually built on that warm presence by sharing updates on her business in her small staff meetings, asking to attend the larger department meetings, and eventually asking how to get promoted to managing director. Sabrina said, "The president told me he would never promote anyone he did not know or have some comfort with."

So how do you get comfortable being selectively vulnerable?

Sabrina shows her self-deprecating sense of humor to her close colleagues. But outside of those few people, she was very shy and avoided contact with the president. She assumed that as a trader, if she made a lot of money for the company, it would lead to her promotion. While the results placed her in the large pool of potentials, her results were no guarantee of promotion. She still had to build trust with the president of the division, who was a weak tie. What changed her comfort level was increased exposure to the president, working up from the regular smiles to informal chats on the trading desk, speaking at the department meetings, and participating in charity events.

Research shows that the top five percent of large organizations lower the risk of these vulnerable acts by conducting them in informal settings, which increases the odds of success. Asking for help or advice does make you vulnerable. However, when done in informal settings in which they're more relaxed, people tend to open up.[44]

Once Sabrina became more comfortable participating in staff meetings, she started asking another colleague, who appeared to be an excellent public speaker, for guidance on how to speak up at the president's meetings. And this in turn spurred her on to make a bigger ask for career guidance from more senior executives.

Once you help others and ask for help, most people feel indebted to return the favor. Marketers even call this the Law of Reciprocity. The easiest way to begin is to start with people you trust and then build up to the people you haven't yet established trust with.

When Sabrina and I started working together, she hadn't recognized that if you want to become more influential, you need two key support mechanisms:

- **Weak tie:** People in your network/work environment who can be helpful and are powerful but are not friends.

- **Strong tie:** People in your network with whom you are friends or have high trust and can be more selectively vulnerable.

What are weak ties, and why are they so critical?

The concept of weak ties was first discovered in the 1960s by Mark Granovetter, a Harvard PhD, who was exploring how male job seekers found their current employment. What was most surprising to Granovetter was how often these job seekers received help from friends of friends—what he called, "weak ties."

These "weak ties" were the links that connected people who were not directly connected by the friendship themselves. It works like this: You tell your friends that you are looking for a job as a web designer, and they hook you up with their running partner who runs a website for a large company.

Granovetter discovered that the weak-tie relationships were often more important than strong-tie friends in giving us access to people, networks, and jobs to which we would not otherwise be connected. Granovetter's research found that while nearly seventeen percent of job seekers heard about a job through a strong tie, almost twenty-eight percent heard about the job from a weak tie. Granovetter said that people with few weak ties were deprived of the latest ideas, news, and opportunities, compared with those who had wider and more weak ties.

This research helps us understand why some people receive more job opportunities or promotions than others. Even if you're the smartest person in the room, the best team manager, or most successful stock trader, research shows that those who spend more time building their network get ahead faster than those who focus on being effective and leading teams.[45]

This concept was taken a step further by Adam Grant, PhD, a professor at The Wharton School, in his 2013 best-selling book, *Give and Take*. Grant found that people tend to fall into three camps: Givers, Takers, and Matchers. He shares research and examples that Givers tend to either reach the top or fall to the bottom at organizations. The reason Givers succeed is that they reconnect over time. Most of us are uncomfortable asking for help, especially from people we don't know. But if you are a Giver who often helps people, others are more likely to help you. This is a form of networking.

How givers succeed

Grant cites Adam Rifkin. Although I had never heard of him, *Fortune* named Adam Rifkin Best Networker in the United States in 2011. He had more LinkedIn connections to the six hundred and forty powerful people on *Fortune's* lists than any other human being. Adam Rifkin is an introverted computer nerd who started KnowNow and later PandaWhale. How did he do all this?

The story began in 1993 when a college student named Graham Spencer teamed up with friends to build Excite, an early Web portal and search engine that quickly became one of the most popular sites on the Internet. In 1998, Excite was purchased for $6.7 billion. In 1999, shortly after selling Excite, Spencer received an email from Adam Rifkin asking for help with funding for an internet start-up. Mr. Spencer agreed to meet with him and connected him with an eventual funder for his new venture. How did this happen?

Adam Rifkin

Early in 1994, Rifkin was a raging fan of the punk rock band Green Day. He created a fan site for the band that drew over one hundred thousand people and helped the band become widely successful.

Graham Spencer was also a punk rock fan. He contacted Rifkin via Rifkin's website and suggested that when people search for punk rock on the Internet, they should find more than Green Day. Rifkin had no idea who Spencer was. Rifkin thought Spencer was just another punk rock fan. Because Rifkin wanted to help the punk scene, he created a separate page on the Green Day fan site with links to the punk rock bands Graham suggested. The page took off.

Rifkin went back to graduate school and lost touch with Spencer.

Five years later, when Rifkin reached out to Spencer, he received help with his start-up. This shows the power of generosity. Givers are more likely to widen their networks—and thus have more chances to get lucky.

The story illustrates that Adam Rifkin is a smart giver and not someone who gives at his own expense. In *Give and Take*, Adam Grant found Givers can be found both at the top and the bottom of the success ladder. The Givers who let others take advantage of them too often never rise to the top. Grant's book makes distinctions among savvy and selfless Givers, Matchers, and Takers.

Givers, Takers, and Matchers

Givers	Takers	Matchers
• Prefer to give more than they get • Other-focused (not selfless) • Help even when the personal costs outweigh the benefits • Strive to be generous with their time, energy, knowledge, skills, ideas, and connections	• Like to get more than they give • Self-focused • Might help when the benefits outweigh the personal costs	• Strive to preserve a roughly equal balance of giving and getting • Operate on the principle of fairness: When they help others, they protect themselves by seeking reciprocity • Believe in tit for tat

Our focus in this book is on identifying and practicing simple Giver actions. I realize some perfectionists may be Takers, others may be Matchers, and others might be selfless Givers. I am not asking you to become a Giver per se; just realize that, when you help others as Adam Rifkin did, it makes it easier to ask for help, and it has the ripple effect. It is easier to win if you turn enemies into allies and help others succeed.[46]

One of my favorite stories that illustrates how giving is cumulative is from *Lean In* by Sheryl Sandberg. It's a true story of how four women rose to reach the ranks of executive officers and managing director level at Merrill Lynch. In 2004, four women started having lunch together once a month. They shared their accomplishments and frustrations. After the lunches, they would all go back to their offices and tout one another's achievements. They couldn't brag about themselves, but they could easily praise their colleagues. Their strategy advanced all of their careers.[47]

I love sharing this story in seminars. The typical response I receive from most women is that they rarely, if ever, practice this type of giving. And yet, they usually all agree that they don't like bragging about themselves. We perfectionists face three challenges in this situation: getting more comfortable asking for help, giving compliments, and accepting compliments.

The three techniques to building a safety net of support

Used consistently, these three tools will build trust more quickly. Beginning at the bottom of the pyramid below, we will describe each one and discuss examples of how to execute each technique with those with whom we have high and low levels of trust. As Sabrina's and the Merrill Lynch stories demonstrate, it takes a village to succeed, and it is safest to start small and build up.[48]

A Model to Build Safety*

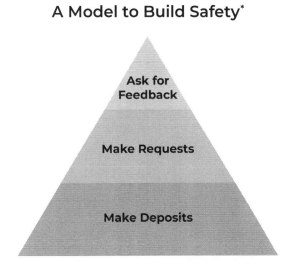

Ask for Feedback

Make Requests

Make Deposits

* Adapted from *Trust Matters—Leadership for Successful Schools* (2004) by Megan Tschannen-Moran, and Jim Roussin, Generative Human Sytems.

- **Make deposits.** Be someone who regularly notices small things and makes deposits and places credits in people's emotional bank accounts.

- **Make requests or ask for help.** Find a middle way to assert your needs while respecting others; alter your approach based on the level of trust.

- **Ask for feedback.** Ask regularly, from those who you respect. The goal is to become more comfortable asking and receiving feedback by starting with those with whom you trust.

Make deposits: make it a way of life

The Emotional Bank Account[49] is a metaphor for the amount of trust that you build up in a relationship. It takes four to seven consistent interactions to change a negative perception.

Stephen Covey suggests these major deposits:

- Understanding the person

- Attending to the little things

- Keeping commitments or promises

- Showing personal integrity

- Apologizing sincerely

- Clarifying expectations

- Offering compliments

Whenever I show the Emotional Bank Account list to a group of women leaders, everyone feels the content is obvious. But when I ask how many of the women give compliments to people that they don't like or don't know, most say they don't do that because it seems sleazy or political. Women prefer to focus on giving compliments to those who deserve it and/or to those with whom they are friends.

In contrast, men may not enjoy "kissing up" to get ahead either, but they're more likely to do it. Men tend to realize that work is like a football team: to win, you need to get along with everyone.

Men tend to focus more on winning versus whether people like them. For example, my husband, Stuart, who works in product development, will regularly bring cookies to meetings with salespeople as a way of creating goodwill. His goal is to get the salespeople to sell his products, especially the new ones. Stuart isn't trying to be best friends with all of them. Rather, he is focused on making deposits and creating more goodwill.

That's why the bank account is such a perfect metaphor for trust, because we all know that you can't take from an empty bank account. And since we're going to make unmistakable withdrawals, we'd better have enough in savings to compensate. For example, when my husband and I were first dating, I would want to arrive at seven thirty for a seven forty-five evening movie, while he would want to arrive around seven to get a good seat. I soon realized the fighting over thirty minutes was needlessly depleting the bank account. Attending to the little things, such as my husband's preference to arrive anywhere very early, is a small deposit. So, now, I happily go thirty minutes early, which makes for a much happier marriage. This strategy also works with your colleagues at work. Always look for ways to give and make trust deposits.

How building the emotional bank account helped Sabrina and Dina

Most deposits take very little time, as Sabrina's story demonstrated. Sabrina just needed to adopt a Giver mindset, constantly seeking every small window to offer a specific compliment or attend to the little things. Sabrina's A-ha moment was realizing that just by being friendlier with the president, she was making a deposit.

Dina, too, struggled to adopt the Giver's mindset. She worried that if she gave too many compliments, she would be perceived as a sycophant. Many of the men she worked with were very competitive and always looking for ways to grab attention. We started small, asking her to use "we" as much as possible in the congratulatory emails. If she accomplished something on her own, she would only send that email to a handful of people. As she started doing this on a regular basis, people started to view her as more of a team player. This was a first step to building trust—but she still needed to learn how and when to ask for help and feedback.

Most women are very good at helping others; they just need to:

- Change their negative mindset.

- Stop viewing it as "kissing up."

- View making deposits in people's emotional bank accounts as an opportunity to leverage their strengths—and see it as a critical part of building and maintaining trust.

Making requests

One of my favorite things is enjoying a frothy hot cup of black tea in the mornings. My husband usually gets up first and makes tea for both of us. One morning, I asked him to bring it into the bedroom. My husband felt like it was a command and expressed his annoyance, letting me know that he was not my servant. Surprised, I hadn't realized that my tone sounded bossy. I have run my own business and been the boss for decades, so I'm used to giving orders. So, especially as a woman, my challenge is how to make a request versus a demand. It's a fine line.

When I attended the Newfield Coaching[50] program in 2010, I was taught how to give a request along with the conditions of satisfaction mentioned earlier. Newfield, an ontological coach training program, changed my life. Suddenly, I had very simple frameworks and techniques to live regeneratively. The words "regenerative" and "request" hadn't been part of my vocabulary before the program. I either commanded or felt needy and asked for help. "Request" seemed like a middle-choice that felt assertive while still respecting others.

The Newfield program is ranked as one of the top coach training programs for those who are looking to do real transformational work. The training involved exploring and revisiting fundamental questions about how you view the world and how that impacts what you generate and achieve. As a result, I broke some old habits of thinking and acting and greatly enhanced my personal well-being, my relationships, and my capacity to create a creative and regenerative professional and personal life. I ended friend relationships that were no longer working for me. I decided to focus on different types of coaching and training assignments. What I really loved about the program was that it was multidisciplinary, bringing in philosophy, biology, various other sciences, cosmology, epistemology, organizational development, sociology, ontology, body movement studies (somatics), and emotional intelligence.

We spent a lot of time on understanding how to manage our emotions and body language. As a former competitive tennis player, I'm very aware of the importance of using your body to achieve certain outcomes. There was a lot of dancing and experimenting with body postures. I realized that I tend to be a warrior. No surprise! So, I've worked on expanding my repertoire to alter my posture as a way of helping me access different emotions, from calm to love to playfulness. I walked away with simple practices, such as learning how to center myself and make sure that my body language matches my actions. This is leading me—and my clients—to live with greater effectiveness, well-being, and satisfaction.

The A-ha for me was to make sure I match my body language with my verbal approach when making requests.

Elements for effective requests[51]
- **Committed speaker.** Demonstrate that you want to make the time for a conversation. Make eye contact while asking someone instead of yelling from another room.

- **Committed listener**. Does not multitask, demonstrates solid eye contact, and is present.

- **Future action and conditions of satisfaction.** Make clear what we want the listener to do (future action) and what standards we want him/her to apply while doing it (conditions of satisfaction). For example, "Can you please make me some tea without the milk?" If you're unsure about the end product (for instance, you don't like your current haircut, but you aren't sure what hairstyle you desire), speak your concerns and declare yourself a beginner.

- **Time frame.** When do we want others to do a task? Sometimes it is obvious and other times it is not. What "as soon as possible" means to one person may be different to another.

- **Mood of the request. The conversation in the wrong mood is the wrong conversation.** Be aware of your mood and the mood of those you talk to. This will impact the meaning and the conversation.

- **Context.** We set the context when we inform the listener of what is going on in the background or what has occurred in the past. This provides perspective on what the request means. For me, the challenge in asking my husband for tea is to NOT make it sound like an army sergeant's command!

The three key points when making requests are:

- **Mood of the request.** I now make this my first thought. Am I in the right mood? Then I make sure my body language and emotions match my mood. I smile and express gratitude when asking my husband for tea.

- **Committed speaker and listener**. I now try to look at my husband and speak while in the same room versus barking at him from the bedroom to make me tea.

- **Conditions of satisfaction.** The clearer this can be the better. What do I really want? This is the game changer. I now ask myself, "What do I really want?" The tea example seems simple, but I've refined it to asking my husband to make tea and put honey in it and then I will put the milk in later, since I stay in bed for another ten to fifteen minutes. Previously, he would make my tea with the milk; it would get cold too quickly, and I would get annoyed.

What these components have taught me is to ask for help in a way that builds trust and doesn't deplete my confidence by making me feel needy—or overcompensate for my own discomfort about asking by becoming bossy.

Of course, in the workplace, sometimes you have to make requests of people you don't know that well. The secret to getting more comfortable with making requests is asking for help differently from those with whom you have low- versus high-trust relationships.

Three stories of making requests

Begin where you have high trust. The stronger the trust, the more the person will accept your mistakes—and the more easily you can build your confidence. Here are three examples of what this looks like with people with whom you have high and low trust.

- First, my own example of starting The Not-Nice Group, in which participants shared challenges and provided honest feedback.

- Second, a story from a client of mine who had to ask her boss for support.

- Third, Fiona and Jill, two women with very diverse styles and approaches who had to learn to work together.

Let's begin with the high-trust example. That's the safer way to begin and build some confidence. Later, you can move on to asking people when you don't have as strong a relationship.

How to make requests with high trust

I began this chapter with an example of asking my husband to make me some tea. It seems simple enough. Yet, as a woman, I find many of my simple requests to my spouse leave me feeling that he sees me as an army general. You may have experienced similar feelings in interactions with your own significant other. How to break out of this trap? Practice. Practice. Practice—with your friends.

A few years ago, I formed a small group with a couple of friends. We agreed to meet once a month over dinner to share what was happening in our lives and make requests. Since our goal was to really get down and dirty with what is happening in our lives versus staying at the surface level, we called ourselves The Not-Nice Group.

Our ground rules provided each participant with fifteen to twenty minutes to share a challenge. Each member of the group would provide honest feedback, ask questions, or request advice. Many times, it would feel harsh—but everyone agreed that the goal was being honest, with compassion. Even so, at first, I found it shockingly hard to ask for advice or guidance. I hated admitting even to my friends that I didn't know what to do or couldn't figure something out. I would rather ask a therapist or figure it out myself.

As we continued to meet over time, I came to look forward to and rely on this group. I could be my authentic self and knew that no matter what I would say or what help I would request, the responses would come from people who had my back. The example in the following chart highlights a current challenge for which I am asking for help. This deep support developed a new level of comfort and patterns of safety around asking for help. And I was able to practice asking my husband for a cup of tea from a place of gratitude, which generated a much warmer approach and was well-received.

	High trust (me)	Low trust (Fiona)
Mood	Gratitude	Confidence
Approach	Warm tone and eye contact	Direct eye contact, slight smile, clear, loud speaking voice.
Conditions of satisfaction	"I need a strategy for talking with my elderly aunt about her living arrangement, which I believe is unsustainable due to her age."	"What information do you want me to include you on from big picture to details that will add to your day? For example, do you want me to CC you on X, Y, and Z or not?

The support reminded me that even in relationships in which there is high trust, it can be uncomfortable to ask for help. While it felt silly, gradually it has become much more comfortable. Success has come from acknowledging my own discomfort, taking a few seconds to get in the right mood, and practice.

This practice of asking for help in everyday life is critical to override many women's aversion to asking for help at work. For example, a client's mother, who was a doctor and working mother of three, taught her, "Any ask is too much." This very direct life-long message caused extra stress when my client, a senior-level lawyer, lost her childcare during the pandemic. Her struggle to find a replacement continuously interrupted her work life. And, just as soon as she had found reliable childcare, it all fell apart, and she had to start all over again. Meanwhile, the company was asking all senior leaders, including her, to start returning to the office.

Although she had a strong relationship with her boss, she loathed the idea that she needed to ask him to let her keep working at home while she resolved her childcare problem. All those messages from her own mother kept getting in the way. She was fearful that her request would label her as someone who is not a team player or committed to the firm. She would have preferred to just suck it up, drop the children off at day care, and go into the office for a few hours a day. But this would add to the craziness of her life and exhaust her.

So, I challenged her. I pointed out that her request could help the leaders to understand that many women were still struggling with childcare; they needed to understand how difficult it was for working mothers with young children. She agreed to ask her boss—and he was very supportive!

How to make requests when there is low trust

I was asked to coach Fiona, a new nursing executive at a large hospital, by her boss, Jill, who was beginning to wonder if she had chosen the wrong person. Fiona had come in with a strong area of expertise but was driving her boss crazy with her endlessly long emails.

Fiona was hired to lead a significant change effort at the hospital. She was highly outgoing, effusive, talkative, and passionate. She was very excited and nervous about taking on this challenge at such a large hospital. Her previous positions had included executive roles in small, regional hospitals and a consulting firm. This was a huge step and a highly political environment, which was new to Fiona.

Jill had worked at the hospital for several decades and quickly realized that Fiona was politically naive and emotionally needy. Fiona was constantly dropping by—saying hello and sending long emails, asking for input. She seemed to require constant positive feedback. Jill had neither the time nor the emotional energy to manage Fiona. I was hired to help Fiona learn how to navigate in this tough and very political environment.

One of the first activities that Fiona and I worked on was to take the FIRO-B self-assessment, which measures how you typically behave with other people and how you expect them to act toward you. Research based on FIRO-B shows that people who make efforts to clarify and align with their manager's approach to working increase trust more quickly. A key part of building that trust is making requests.

I've used the FIRO-B for about twenty years. It's a quick way to gain insights into what motivates you and what drains your energy at work. The FIRO-B model provides a simple sequence to identify and diagnose relationship challenges.[52] It offers a prescriptive approach for steps to building a new relationship, fixing problems, or working effectively with people you don't like—or just struggle to work with.

Building Stronger Trust

PERFECTIONIST	EMOTIONAL BANK ACCOUNT
Fiona tries to give her boss, Jill, everything via frequent, lengthy, and detailed updates and focuses on doing her job well.	Fiona notices her new boss, Jill, sends two-to-three-word emails; she asks how Jill wants to be included, what formats work best, and how to handle urgent matters. She focuses on doing a good job.
Her boss doesn't reply to most long emails, sends short emails, and never gives Fiona positive feedback.	Jill asks Fiona to cc on a few key items, brief bullet-format weekly updates, and schedule calls for urgent matters.

PERFECTIONIST	EMOTIONAL BANK ACCOUNT
Fiona feels unsure if she is doing a good job; Jill tells the coach that she is wondering if Fiona can handle this new role.	Fiona's boss starts thanking Fiona for her updates, replies to her brief weekly updates, helps her solve problems, and tells her she is doing a good job.

As you review the previous chart, you can see what was happening to Fiona as she attempted to build trust with Jill. Because Fiona's approach was so annoying to Jill, her entire credibility was questioned. This was a huge learning moment for Fiona, as she'd never experienced such a challenge to her self-esteem. The turning point in the relationship came when Fiona started accepting the negative impact her approach was having on her relationship with her boss. The rub is usually that most people feel it seems so unfair that they have to morph into someone else. The reality is that all Fiona needed to do was to observe her boss and make some simple requests:

"I notice you send brief emails, and I send long ones. I want to understand how to best work with you, so I enhance your day versus annoy you. I want to figure out ways of working together that will be satisfying and productive."

Here are five key requests that will help build trust more quickly with a new working relationship[53]

- What information do you want me to pass on to you—from big picture to details? For example, do you want me to cc you on X, Y, and Z, or not?

- How often do you want to be included on the big picture/details—monthly, weekly, daily?

- What communication formats are best for big picture, details, and emergencies? For example: Do you want me to call you only in emergencies and otherwise send you bulleted updates every week? What decisions can I make independently? Which ones do you want to be included on?

- What are your pet peeves?

The biggest challenge for Fiona was to manage her body language and stay confident without becoming too effusive. This took practice. But, once Jill and Fiona had the conversation and started working together differently, trust began to be built, and Fiona's confidence increased.

How you make the request is crucial in low-trust relationships. You need to ask from a place of confidence and focus on identifying ways to build trust. Once you have high trust, you can get away with more—and the how matters less.

Now that you've become more comfortable asserting yourself, we'll move to asking for feedback, which can be the most challenging and yet the most essential if you want to continue to grow.

Asking for feedback

Seeking out feedback was a way of life in my tennis world. Even though, as a perfectionist, I didn't really want it, I was able to take it because I hired a tennis coach I trusted, and she would give direction to me in a private and compassionate manner. My skills as a tennis player improved, which in turn made me want to seek out more feedback. Research shows that if constructive feedback on your performance/actions is given in an appropriate manner, performance improves.[54]

The key to breaking the shackles of perfectionism is to build up feedback resilience, so you become less emotional and react more confidently. The strategy is to start asking for positive and constructive feedback more often. As I described earlier, females tend to receive mostly positive feedback growing up and can be too trusting of other's opinions of them. Women need to learn to be more discerning about whom and how they ask.

When I started working in a large competitive organization in the 1990s, I quickly realized that no news was good news. And, as a woman who worked in the male-dominated investment banking field, I also witnessed how rarely men gave women feedback. Sadly, this continues today. Asking for feedback as a working woman is tricky business.

Many of my women coaching clients come to me because no one has given them constructive feedback. When I ask male leaders why, many will say, "I don't want to make her cry," or "I am too afraid of a lawsuit." I once was offered a coaching assignment to a woman who had gained weight after having children, and her clothes were too tight. All the senior leaders in the company were male, including the head of HR who'd hired me—and they didn't want to tell her to buy new clothes.

Luckily things have changed a lot, especially once Millennials became the largest group in the workplace. Generation Z is starting to transition into the workplace, which means they are steeped in learning process. They have different expectations regarding feedback

Millennial/Generation Y (1981-1996):[55]
- Expect to receive feedback regularly and frequently.

- Need positive feedback more frequently and less formally.

Generation Z (1996 and later)[56]
- Love constant feedback—good or bad.

- Good feedback fuels them to redouble their efforts in their jobs.

What is feedback, why it is challenging for perfectionists, and how does one get comfortable asking for it?

There's abundant literature out there about how to seek and give performance feedback. I want to first focus on defining feedback and then provide simple tactics for us perfectionists to get comfortable asking people we respect.

The chart shows that effective feedback is observable facts—not opinions or judgments. It's about things that you *can* change. The comedian John Cleese of Monty Python has made many corporate training videos. I used them in teaching feedback. There's one I'll never forget, a hilarious example of how not to give feedback. Instead of telling a man he needed to lose weight, a doctor tells him at his annual physical, "You are a foot too short."

The goal is to give feedback in a way that makes the person want to take ownership and make the changes out of personal motivation, *not* just to comply. For this to happen, the person has to accept the feedback—and thus, the feedback provider has to give that feedback in ways that work for the recipient.

Giving and receiving feedback appropriately are among the biggest challenges for perfectionists, especially women. Because perfectionists tend to define themselves by what they do, feedback can feel like a personal attack. So the way to build your feedback resilience at work is to start small and make it safe.

FEEDBACK IS	FEEDBACK IS NOT
• Information that enables you to develop or improve your performance, usually given after an event or performance.	• Necessarily negative.
	• A one-way monologue.
• Focused on ownership change.	• About things that cannot be changed.
• Can be positive or constructive.	• An opportunity for a personal attack.
• "When you don't respond to my request within 24 hours, I can't complete the order, and we might lose the business."	• An opinion unsupported by observation or data.
	• "You seem like you don't care when you don't respond to my request within 24 hours."

In today's fast-moving world, asking for and receiving both positive feedback about things done well and constructive feedback showing how to do better is critical. If you want people to receive and be open to accepting constructive feedback, you need to create and nurture a positive emotional bank account. So, if you're a manager, give three positives for every negative. It is important to ask for—and give—detailed positive feedback (not just a vague "good job") *before* giving constructive feedback with specific suggestions for improvement, delivered in ways that maintain the self-esteem of the listener. This is one of any manager's most important tasks.

For example, a manager of my newly promoted coaching client in the fashion industry, Daria, wanted to give feedback that would help Daria communicate more effectively in large meetings. The manager had previously told her to stop taking notes and speak up more. This had not led to a change of behavior.

I suggested beginning with positive feedback—telling Daria that when she speaks up, she adds a lot of value because of her strong fashion sensibility and knowledge. And, that her team valued the breadth of information she brought to the table, which in turn was essential to making higher quality decisions.

Once Daria understood the impact of her actions, we were able to work on ways for her to feel comfortable speaking up more often while still listening and retaining the essential points at the meeting.

How to make asking for feedback safe

I created the acronym MAATT to help women get comfortable asking for feedback. It uses five simple steps to increase the likelihood of getting useful feedback.

MOOD. Come from a place of confidence and curiosity, not weakness; the right conversation in the wrong mood is the wrong conversation.

ASK. Ask people that you respect. Reach out to a diverse group, including those with whom you have high and low trust. Vary the approach depending on the level of trust. Ask for both positive and constructive feedback.

AVOID. Avoid being defensive.

THANK. Thank people for their feedback.

TELL. Offer people a story about how you applied their feedback and its impact.

Tactics for asking those with whom you have high and low trust

Ask people that you respect and from whom you want feedback. Start wherever is easiest for you. Vary the tactics depending on the level of trust.

Asking for feedback

	High Trust (me)	Low Trust (Dina)
Approach	Ask the person if you both can agree to offer each other candid feedback; agree to provide one area to improve at a time; and look for ways to offer more positives.	Build relationships by offering compliments such as, "I know some of you have extensive experience in X, and I would appreciate your insights" or by asking questions, "Curious, who has done Y?"
Tactic	Ask the person ahead of time if they can provide positive and constructive feedback after a presentation you give.	Post the facts—positive and negative; comment that you realize the results could be stronger AND that you would value their feedback—what recommendations do they have.
Follow-up	Thank the person and discuss how you can continue to support each other.	Thank the group or person and update them on how you used the feedback.

How to ask for feedback from a person with whom you have high trust

I asked Ann, a fellow coach, to attend my first presentation on the material in this book and provide me with feedback by observing me with the audience, noticing what people responded to and what didn't work. I've known Ann for over twenty years, and I respect and trust her completely.

Ann and I met after my presentation, and she offered me a list of specific aspects that went well and two areas that could be improved. She helped me realize that my stories, the interaction, and the exercises were all engaging. But I needed to start with one of the entertaining stories and provide more specific instructions for the main exercise. I incorporated these changes into future programs and shared the results with Ann.

How to ask for feedback from a person with whom you have low trust

Earlier, we met Dina, who worked on the mostly male trading desk and tried to self-promote by sending emails about her accomplishments. As part of my work with her, I interviewed a few senior executives about her performance and prospects of getting promoted. The most surprising comment was from a male executive, Bart. He liked her monthly updates on the successes that she shared. But he observed that Dina only shared successes and never asked for feedback or asked for help when things didn't go so well.

Dina wasn't providing regular updates, only posting positive results. This left Bart and other senior leaders to suspect her accomplishments. They assumed that when months went by without an update, that Dina's business was not posting strong results. Bart's advice was that Dina needed to provide monthly updates—through good times and bad.

When I shared Bart's feedback, Dina was dumbfounded. She'd been working to get promoted and didn't want to look weak. Many of the men on the email list were in competition with her for promotion. She felt that sharing downbeat results might be used against her. But Dina realized that building trust with colleagues involves learning how to make requests and ask for feedback in a smart way, so you don't look weak. Rather, you make your colleagues look good—and possibly turn them into allies.

Dina agreed to post monthly updates, have more regular conversations with key stakeholders, including her competitive peers, and ask for feedback or make requests. This has resulted in a closer working relationship with Dan, a more senior level trader and crucial colleague.

Dina and Dan had a cooperative working relationship, but it hadn't been very open. Dina knew that Dan could mentor her. She asked for a monthly thirty-minute business development, brainstorming, and feedback meeting with Dan. Dan eventually opened up and offered more constructive feedback and ideas. Dina realized that she needed to initiate the feedback process.

Now, she's creating a new business plan in a more inclusive and savvy manner. The next step is to share the plan, with Dan's help, and ask the head of the office some questions. Because she has included Dan in the process, the head of the office and Bart, Dan's boss, will start to view Dina as more influential. It all started with small acts of asking for input.

Wrap-up and transition to strategic networking

We all want to be seen, heard, and valued. All conversations have some level of risk. As perfectionists, we want people to have a favorable impression of us and our work. That can keep us from taking that risk and asking for help.

What has helped me is remembering that when I make a request or ask for feedback or offer to help someone, I am building a wide net of support for myself. Even a tiny gesture like sending a thank-you email to someone's boss for their great work makes it easier to ask for constructive feedback later. I don't have to reveal my fears that people might think my ideas are terrible. The more deposits I make, the easier it is to be seen, heard, and valued. You'll likely find the same positive outcomes as you begin making those goodwill deposits.

Now that you know how to build trust, we'll focus on the final step: strategic networking. Make sure that you're spending time with people who can help you achieve success at your current job and move you toward your larger career goals.

Strategic networking: common problem for women

When I was twenty-nine years old, I had just changed careers from social worker to talent development in a large global bank. I'd become friendly with Jim, a more senior HR professional in the recruiting department. He told me I needed to be more visible with the head of HR, Jeff. I remember telling Jim that if I just worked hard, that would be good enough. Besides, who had time to drop by, and what would I say to Jeff? As a young woman, I'd thought he seemed like a weird dude—and he was old. Yes, I'm embarrassed to admit that was how I thought. But as I've focused on developing women leaders over the last thirty years, I realize that this is not uncommon.

Research shows that women tend to have smaller, close-knit networks made up of people they like, which makes it more challenging for women to be visible.[57] I wanted to spend time with Jim, not Jeff. Since I didn't understand how I could connect with Jeff in an authentic manner, I avoided building a relationship. I didn't realize that I could build a relationship with Jeff just by trying to find something in common, which would require more work on my part, since I was the junior person.

I couldn't see why Jeff would want to have a relationship with me.

What did I have to offer Jeff? Looking back now, I realize that all I would have had to do was to ask some questions and listen to figure out something we have in common or cared about. I am sure I could have found something and that a relationship with him might have helped my career through advice, connections, or feedback.

Why strategic networking is so critical for women in today's world

In today's fast-moving world, we can't possibly keep up or know everything. And no one navigates life's challenges alone. But research finds women are more likely than men to receive unsolicited advice.[58] Therefore, women need to be clear whose advice they value and whose they do not.

What matters is having trusted relationships with the right people, so you can ask someone to advocate for you when you need help. Sylvia Ann Hewlett, author of (Forget a Mentor) Find a Sponsor advises women to acquire a sponsor (a powerfully positioned champion), rather than a mentor (an informal sounding board). She found that sponsors make a measurable difference in helping protégés advance—by connecting them to important people, the right assignments, and critical feedback. The sponsors promote and expect loyalty and stellar performance—and, in turn, they look good. If you want to advance into more senior leadership, you might need a sponsor.[59]

Depending on your career ambition and stage in life, this may or may not be relevant. What everyone needs is a robust network—just as every company needs a board of directors (see the many good books on networking I've listed in the bibliography). Our focus here is on helping you identify whom you want in your strategic network.

What is a strategic network?

Strategic network = increased safety

- Build relationships with a wide range of people with whom you have varied levels of trust, ranging from learning interactions to powerful alliances. These interactions can be formal or informal.

- The goals are to increase your current effectiveness on the job, expand your influence, and support your professional growth and long-term career success..

- Your strategic network provides you with information, guidance, connections, new ideas, and has your back when you make mistakes or need help.

As you can see, the goal is to have people who have your back who can help you now and in the future. To achieve this, you need to connect with the right people, at varying levels of trust. This network gives us more freedom to stretch outside of our comfort zones, ask for feedback, and gain knowledge.

How does increased safety help you succeed?

When I was writing my first book, *Collaborative Competition: A Woman's Guide to Succeeding by Competing*, I interviewed forty women in highly competitive professions. My goal was to discover differences between women who succeeded and those who stumbled. The critical finding was that sixty percent of the women who succeeded in tough, male-dominated professions such as politics or investment banking were better at building strategic networks than other women. These two women highlight the differences.[60]

Jane was one of the most successful women I interviewed. She moved from teaching to a C-suite financial services executive. How did she do it? She was smart and hard-working. But her strategy was to build a strong network. She was always looking for ways to make deposits in people's emotional bank accounts—to make people look good or help them. These strong relationships enabled her to take on roles outside of her expertise. While she didn't have an economics or finance background, she was able to step beyond her comfort zone because people trusted her. Once women take a risk and succeed, and they have a strong network, they are more likely to continue to be offered ever-expanding roles. This strategy of making deposits, building a strong network of trusted advisors while working hard and being a quick study enabled Jane to succeed.

In contrast, Clare's story tells a different but more common tale. When I met Clare, she'd recently lost her job. She met me wearing sweatpants, as she was going to work out after our meeting. Losing her job had been a real wake-up moment that had led her to make significant life changes, including getting back into shape.

Clare had been a top law school graduate and had always prided herself on excelling at work. She had moved up quickly within the legal department and was appointed general counsel at a relatively young age. Work had been her entire life. She had the strong support of the COO, who helped promote her. But when the COO lost his job in a merger, Clare didn't have any other critical allies. Once the new CEO came in, she put her head down and worked even harder, hoping that her excellent work and reputation would help her keep her job. She didn't know who else to turn to, as she disliked networking and asking for help. She soon lost her job. Realizing that hard work and past successes were not enough was a tough and painful lesson.

So—how can you build the right network, so your career is more like Jane's and less like Clare's?

What does the ideal network look like?

Clare and Jane's stories explain why it is so important to be building the right network. Most people don't realize how important networks are until they are in Clare's position and really need help. But by then, it's often too late. There are a lot of myths about networking,[61] such as:

- Only extroverts are good networkers.

- Networking is insincere or manipulative.

- It takes too much time.

And so on.

Research on those who have strong networks, such as Jane, has found that success is more about intention than skill. And, as we have discussed, networking is more about giving and building trusting relationships first. The biggest mistake I see many women and leaders making is that their networks are too small, and they spend most of their time with people they're already comfortable with.

Research by Robert Cross from his book, *Driving Results through Social Networks*, co-authored by Robert Thomas, found that High Performers' success is linked to their ability to form high-quality relationships with people who are strategic to their careers/success.[62]

The adjectives "high-quality" and "strategic" mean different things to different people. These contacts don't have to be your best friends, which is where I think women get stuck. Instead, these contacts need to be people you can learn from, who can broaden your perspectives, connect you with others, and help you grow your career. In today's complex, decentralized organizations, your networks are what ensure that you are driving performance and innovation. And if you want to take on broader responsibilities, research shows you need different types of people in your network.[63] Review the following list. We'll discuss each type and let you reflect on your own network so you can develop an action plan.

The Ideal Network

Type	Purpose	Location, Attributes, and Key Behaviors
Day-to-day work/go-to people	Colleagues you reach out to regularly to get work done	These contacts are mostly internal; they are knowledgeable about the tasks and organizational structure.
Personal (friends)	People with whom you have high trust; provide support, professional development, and useful information/contacts	Mostly external but can be internal
Competent jerks[64]	Challenge your thinking and minimize insularity	These people are usually internal; they have an area of expertise that is valued and can have low social skills.
Strategic manager/ mentor/sponsor	Provide longer-term guidance, assist with gaining support for career moves	Internal and external, with a focus on the future and knowledge of the bigger picture and/or organization
Peers who have different areas of expertise and approaches who can extend your abilities, areas of expertise, and approaches	Expand your thinking, expand collaboration across silos, and increase innovation productivity	Internal and external; people you like and seek out because of their expertise and diverse perspectives

Type	Purpose	Location, Attributes, and Key Behaviors
Group that interests you outside of your immediate work group	Expand your visibility, break down organizational silos	Groups need to be interested in you and/or willing to help you gain useful connections beyond your current work situation such as an employee affinity network,65 industry organization, charitable organizations, or an alumni network

Why are competent jerks on the list?

That is a smart question. In my first book, *Collaborative Competition: A Woman's Guide to Succeeding by Competing,* I encourage women to find pacing partners, people who can bring out the best in them. This comes from the world of sports; to become a great athlete, you need to practice with people who challenge you. If you're always the winner, you're not growing. That is the idea behind having at least one competent jerk in your network. It also comes from the research, which found that if people have a choice between lovable fools and competent jerks, they prefer to work with lovable fools. Therein lies the problem. Perfectionists, because of our desire to win and look good, struggle with this concept of having challengers in their network.

In my own efforts, I started simple: looking for challengers who can beat me on the tennis court. As I've become more comfortable with playing against people who are as good if not better than me, it has given me confidence to seek out peer mentors and others with whom I can learn from and grow. Start small.

When I lead seminars in large companies, I often encounter women who never consciously thought about seeking to challenge themselves through forming a better relationship with a competent jerk. But once they learn that there might be something to be gained and that the relationship can be built in safely, they agree to experiment in a simple way, such as offering an annoying colleague a compliment and then asking her for guidance on something she does well.

Building your strategic network

The first step is to assess the strong relationships you already have—and identify potential gaps. There is no perfect network. It will depend a lot on your level, role, and ambition. The focus of this exercise is on understanding who is in your inner circle. Who do you seek out? For what? Do you have enough of the right people to help you at your current job and to support your continued growth? How many people come to mind: Five? Eight? Ten? Fifteen? More? Answer the following questions.

A strategic approach to expanding your network: exercise

Develop an action plan—start where you are and identify one tiny action you can take regularly.

List five to ten people you consider part of your network—people with whom you have some trust. You might only see your mentor once or twice a year, but that relationship is critical. Think about these questions:

Who do you spend time with? What's the purpose of the interaction? Do you get information from them? Do you enjoy their company? Do you trust their advice? What's your level of trust with them?

Robert Cross observed that many people will spend more time with people they like than with people who have information they need and/or can help them grow their career.[66]

Often, that comes as a shock. The first time I did this, I realized I needed to expand my relationships and include people who have some important business advice—and not just ask my close friend who ran a successful business.

Name	Purpose/Role	Level of Trust—Low, Medium, High

Review the key stakeholders in your network.

Visualize your ideal network among people you already know. Who do you need a stronger relationship with to help you be more effective? Who can help your long-term career growth?

Identify one or two key stakeholders with whom you would like to build a stronger relationship. What one or two actions can you take?

Real example—how Sabrina built her network

When I asked Sabrina to do this exercise, her network was very small. There were less than five people in her trusted network, and they were either peers or junior staff. She had a decent relationship with her boss and was beginning to get to know the president of her division. But she barely knew the two senior women leaders in her division, was not involved in any groups outside of her direct responsibilities, and, therefore, had few cross-department relationships.

Her gap? The biggest gap in her network was lack of visibility with senior leaders in the organization. She understood that to get promoted to managing director (MD), she would have to be known by the president and a few other key senior leaders.

The other big challenge was that she viewed networking as inefficient and a waste of time. She was a trader and focused on managing her bottom line. She was not on LinkedIn and only went to networking events when it was a client event, or she felt she could not get out of it. On top of it all, she loathed public speaking. But she was told that if she wanted to become a managing director, she would need to focus on growing the profits of the larger organization. What helped her get her head around networking was realizing that by expanding her trust circle, she could grow the bottom line through identifying potential business deals and getting things done more efficiently for clients.

Actions for Sabrina in building a stronger network

As I described earlier, we focused on three actions:

- Being friendly with the president of the organization. Saying hello to him, speaking up at his meetings, and sharing weekly updates on her business.

- Reaching out to a senior-level woman leader with whom she was friendly, but she'd never asked for guidance around the MD process. She asked this woman to have coffee.

- Getting involved in a large charity that supported under-privileged children. As a mother herself, she cared about giving back in her community. All the senior leaders of the bank were involved with this charity, which held regular events throughout the year. She volunteered at one event, which allowed her to have informal conversations with a broader group of leaders.

As a result of these tiny actions steps, she became more visible. Her network grew from fewer than five trusted advisors to more than ten within a year. The relationships she formed were critical to her promotion to MD.

Sabrina realized that she didn't have to become a sycophant to be a strategic networker. She just needed to see networking as critical to her job and making a larger impact.

Wrap-up

Networking has been given a bad name. As perfectionists, we care about getting results. The web of support you build and maintain is the safest way to get there. If you want people to listen to your advice and implement your brilliant ideas, then you need to take baby steps to start expanding and strengthening your network. Begin with your friends and friendly colleagues.

Have a beer with your friend and ask how everyone seems to know them. Ask that colleague who always has to be right and is more knowledgeable than you about something for advice. You might be pleasantly surprised.

Shackle-smashing actions

The aim of this chapter is to make the risk-taking process easier and more efficient. The more connected you are, the more supported you will feel. Risk-taking becomes less risky because you're building a net around you. Start by adding some tiny actions to your to-do lists—and before you know it, they'll become new habits, and those old chains will fall to the ground!

What's one small step you can take to break out of those shackles?

- The easiest way I have found to expand my network beyond my comfort zone is to be a volunteer mentor for the Financial Women's Association. The program provides roughly forty mentors—successful professional women—for top women college students in business during their junior and senior years. Making a deposit by supporting these young women makes it more comfortable to build relationships with new people. I've started asking one or two of the mentors to have a coffee or lunch, as people open up more in informal settings. What is the easiest way for you to expand your network? How can you leverage the deposits you are already making?

- Another easy way is to offer assistance to a key stakeholder; for example, I'm an avid reader of the *Harvard Business Review* and MIT's *Sloan Management Review*. I am always looking to send articles or post them on LinkedIn. Where do your interests lie? And how can you use those special passions to help others?

What is one small physical action you can take to break out of those shackles?

- I work virtually, so I have a large wall mirror near my desk that reminds me to smile more often—especially when I'm networking on the phone or on Zoom. This is important, as smiling softens your voice.

- My go-to approach to calm myself and my clients down is to take five deep breaths that begin at my belly rather than at my throat; I do this in between meetings or while at a networking meeting to calm down and collect my thoughts.

Now that you've learned the main tools to becoming a more resilient perfectionist in the 21st century, let's end with dessert—how to lighten up and actually enjoy it all.

CHAPTER 10

Action 5: Lighten Up

"Happiness takes energy and discipline, and it is easy to be heavy and hard to be light."

Gretchen Rubin, *The Happiness Project*[67]

This quote saved my vacation and my relationship with my husband while on an adventure in Cambodia. Given that I was a tennis champion as a child, I'd always taken my athletic challenges to heart. As perfectionists, we also tend to take ourselves seriously. We are always striving to improve, do it faster or better.

But what happens if you're always aiming too high and have rigid standards? I found the answer the hard way.

Keep in mind as you read through this adventure that this kind of mindset shift is your key to smashing the shackles of perfectionism in any situation, not just in an athletic challenge. It illustrates most of the key principles we've been exploring, and it applies in the work environment, in a family situation, or just any situation that creates a clash of expectations and achievements. Thus, I've gone into some detail. Think of it as a case study from my own life—a situation where I applied productive reframing and assessed real, versus imagined, needs to smash the shackles of my own perfectionism.

And I'd love to hear your success stories, too. Who knows—maybe

I'll be asking your permission to include your story in a future book.

I found myself in ninety-plus-degree heat on a rocky, dusty road in Cambodia, riding a bicycle along with my husband and a couple of fellow travelers from Australia. Hot and exhausted, I thought, "What am I doing? I am not training for 'Survivor' or the Tour de France! This is supposed to be an adventure vacation, which means a rest from work. Well, this is no rest."

I am in my fifties. I heard that little negative voice saying, "Don't wimp out. You're getting older, and your comfort zone is shrinking. You should keep riding. If you quit now, you are going to become three O's—old, overweight, and out of shape!"

There it was: The should. The long list of shoulds is a perfectionist's best friend—and worst nightmare.

I was becoming really angry at my husband. Biking was his idea. I decided to stop pedaling and ride in the air-conditioned van to the lunch restaurant. The other three riders told me they weren't enjoying the ride either. But, of course, they didn't stop riding. My husband is a former marathon runner and enjoys long, challenging rides. The Australian couple is from the western city of Perth, and their idea of a good time is camping, hiking, and biking for weeks.

I'm not like them. I enjoy riding for a couple of hours, stopping to have lunch and possibly a beer, then taking a nap in the afternoon. And I don't like camping.

I started to feel a wave of shame and embarrassment come over me at lunch as I realized that I was in a league of my own. No one seemed to care that I got into the van but me, yet I was feeling peer pressure. I obviously had some kind of outdated notion that if I didn't keep pushing on, I was a wimp. This felt like heavy baggage along for the ride with me in Cambodia. I couldn't believe it! Hadn't I evolved past this?

I returned to my hotel that afternoon and cried. My husband and I fought. I was sad, angry, and annoyed. He suggested I should go home. He told me he was sick of my complaining, that I needed to lighten up. I fought back and said I need a little compassion from him. I felt imprisoned within this story that I was only worthy if I was an athletic gladiator. Intellectually, I knew this was silly—but it felt stuck inside of my body.

I knew I wouldn't enjoy the trip unless I chose to let my story go. I meditated, wrote out my feelings, and did therapy on myself. I happened to be reading *The Happiness Project* and realized that I was going to have to be disciplined and focus on making myself happy.

One of my proudest achievements in my life is that I've been able to shed most of the baggage from my troubled childhood. But all children learn both good and bad habits from their parents. On that hot, steamy afternoon in Cambodia, I realized to my horror that I'd adopted my father's unattractive habit of endless complaining. In other words, I'd become annoying. I was suffering from the heat and side effects of malaria medication. But the real pain point was accepting that I was causing my own suffering.

I was overcome by deep sobbing, realizing my identity was still too narrowly defined. My dysfunctional childhood was about seeking love through athletic achievement—which was never celebrated but rather squashed by my narcissistic father. So, instead of enjoying my athletic talents, it felt like an unlucky diagnosis.

Birth of the Happy Warrior

With nine days left on the trip, I finally decided I wanted to be as happy as was possible in a sweltering third-world country, full of bad roads and unsanitary conditions.

I love adventure and admire my husband's positive attitude. But I accepted that my identity needed lightening up. Instead of the Gladiator, I decided to be the Happy Warrior. I accepted that I was a fifty-five-year-old woman in reasonable shape who hadn't trained to bike five-plus hours a day in ninety-plus heat on roads full of potholes. Instead, I started behaving like that Happy Warrior. I only rode in the morning for one to two hours and then spent the rest of the day in the air-conditioned van, listening to my favorite music or taking a nap.

I accepted that those in the group, including my husband, were probably going to tough it out—but I was not going to feel ashamed or less-then about myself because I was taking the easy way out. My husband was delighted and proud of me. The Australians were accustomed to temperatures of over one hundred degrees, and they were not letting the heat stop them. Though they occasionally took a turn in the van, more often, they muscled through. This left me riding in the van for hours by myself with the Cambodian driver, quiet and mild-mannered Mr. Tree.

He and I developed a friendly relationship. He was one of those people who knows what you need before you do. He quickly realized after the first day I rode with him that I needed liquids and an occasional rest stop. We periodically stopped to take pictures of the beautiful Cambodian rice fields, visit temples resting on hilltops, or examine barbequed tarantulas on the side of the road. At the end of each day, when we reached our destination and the other bicycle riders were hot, dirty, and appeared exhausted, I stepped out of the van with a smile on my face, ready to explore the latest town.

A couple of days after shedding the Gladiator and giving myself permission to be the Happy Warrior, I felt freer and lighter. While in the past, the only option I saw had been to trudge on regardless of how I felt, I instead saw many options. And I've learned to feel compassion for myself and others. Earlier in the trip, I'd felt like I was left out or envious of others who surpassed me or pushed on.

But as I started to feel happier, I was glad that my fellow riders were enjoying themselves while I didn't have to bicycle in ninety-plus-degree heat. My self-worth and happiness were not linked to my performance. Rather, they were linked to what felt good for me based on my own standards—not those imposed upon me by my parents or by my own impossible standard of perfection.

The last day of the bicycle trip was spent in a gorgeous park full of tall leafy trees, abundant birds, and monkeys swinging between the trees. The roads had been newly paved and were shaded by the towering trees. I felt the urge to ride for the entire morning, as the conditions were perfect. Much to my surprise, the Australian couple was too exhausted and declined to ride. My husband and I spent several hours riding peacefully with no cars in sight and only the sounds of monkeys and birds playing in the wild. This felt like sweet revenge for the hours in the van.

This trip to Cambodia, which took me outside of my environment and comfort zone, helped me see how my standards were self-imposed and that my attachment to unattainable performance was beyond my conscious awareness.

While I'm always encouraging my clients to get out of their comfort zones—and I, too, follow my own advice—this awareness still caught me by surprise.

What is the "so what" here?

My Cambodian adventure loosened the noose around my neck. I no longer had to be that Gladiator at all costs. "Research shows that the more elements that make up your identity, the less threatening it is when any one element is threatened."[68] I now have more options available to me. I am taking my athletic identity less seriously. So what if I don't want to go biking today? Take a day off from exercise! In the past, I would be fearful, beat myself up, and feel shame that I was some sort of wimp.

Shame comes when you feel that you are not worthy of love and belonging because you have not lived up to some standard that is accepted or valued by an important group of people. In the past, I would have felt ashamed meeting the group later after spending the afternoon napping in the comfortable air-conditioned van. Shame, as Brené Brown notes in her book, *Daring Greatly,* can be a killer. It dampens your spirit, creativity, freedom. Shame is powerful because human beings are hardwired for connection.[69] I realized that I was moving towards more wholehearted living, which meant I was becoming more shame resilient. Emerging from the air-conditioned van while the other bikers looked hot and exhausted, I could say to myself, "I am enough, I am worthy of love and belonging." This was a huge breakthrough for me.

How does this ability to laugh off expectations with a joyful "so what?" help you become more productive?

In the workplace, always being focused on the work can hurt results, too.

The following chart highlights the two most common situations I see in working with women.

The "So What" of Lightening Up

BEHAVIOR	IMPACT
You always talk about work with key colleagues, and you only show your fun side at the holiday party.	Key colleagues can't connect with you. During a 360 on you, these colleagues say you can be difficult to work with and ask why the playful person they saw at the holiday party never shows up at work.
You are conscientious about your responsibilities at home and at work	You can't let go of any task—no matter how small—until it's completed exactly as you wanted, rarely delegate or give yourself time off from motherhood, family, and work responsibilities. You feel heavy and resentful at times.

Let's discuss the first example. A common phenomenon I see when I conduct 360-degree interviews for high-potential or C-suite women with their mostly male colleagues is that many people, especially men, can have difficulty connecting with these women who are either always talking about work or never show their light or fun side on the job.

For example, when I conducted interviews for a high-potential female insurance executive, Amy, the overwhelming feedback was that her mostly male colleagues wanted to see some of the woman they'd engaged with at the holiday party at work. Her male colleagues wanted to work with the Amy who had a sense of humor and seemed playful, not the one at work who was very driven and always serious. As the saying goes, humor is the fastest way to build connections.

Amy was surprised and a little offended by these findings. She believed that to be taken seriously in a male-dominated environment, she could not show much of her personal and feminine side. She was afraid to be vulnerable and show any weakness. But once Amy realized that showing more of her warmer side was a positive, not a weakness, she started lightening up more at work. This led her to focus more on building a stronger network of relationships, which helped her get promoted.

We'll discuss the second example at the end of the Stop Should-ing All Over Yourself exercise.

Having been overly serious myself, I understand why women believe they must be serious at work—especially when they work with men. Women have had to work harder and tend to get promoted based on performance, while men often get promoted based on potential.

So, if women want to rise up in this more male-dominated, highly competitive world, they need to prove themselves by working hard. But this is not enough, especially in male-dominated environments. They also need to loosen up a bit and bring a lighter, more playful side to work. As I shared earlier, Sheryl Sandberg cites in *Lean In* that her research shows that as women rise up, they are liked less. Meanwhile, men who exhibit similar traits are viewed more positively. This means women must also work at being perceived as likable. One way to do this is to be selectively vulnerable, as we discussed in the previous chapter. This chapter is focused on how women can bring more of that lighter and playful side to work—and how this will make it easier and less stressful to get work done and connect faster.

How to lighten up without going to Cambodia

The A-ha for me is that even though I engaged in extensive talk therapy that drastically improved my life, it was also essential to work with my body. During the ten-day adventure, I let go of an outdated identity that I had been working to free myself from for decades. Don't worry—my psychotherapy was not wasted. Rather, my self-awareness created a strong foundation to help me reap the benefits of doing a physical activity outside of my comfort zone.

As we discussed earlier, our comfort zone shrinks with age. If, for example, you're a downhill skier, you may not want to venture onto double black diamonds any longer. But that might also be wise; by avoiding those slopes, you reduce the risk of injury and can have a longer skiing career.

The purpose of lightening up is to examine our shoulds—our standards. Check to see if you have some unexamined standards defining and limiting your options—just as I did. Once you are aware of them, you can answer one of my favorite coaching questions: How is that working for you? Then, you can decide if you want to replace those limiting standards with energizing ones, using your wisdom.

This practice builds upon the first habit of cultivating joy. Joy can be related to or independent of events. Joy can be cultivated when you celebrate an accomplishment—or you can just enjoy watching the sunset. The idea is to select activities that you would enjoy and that will lighten you up. Since we perfectionists tend to be doers, we need activities in our lives that loosen us up so that we don't take ourselves so seriously all the time.

Two ways to lightening up

- **Stop should-ing all over yourself and start living.** Examine your "shoulds"—your standards of perfectionism that guide your life. If they're holding you back, replace them with new, more energizing stories.

- **Start an activity to loosen up.** Playful activities make you happier and can help you to be more productive and creative. Select an activity that you either are curious about because it seems like fun or one in which you don't need to excel—and which will bring out your silly creative side.

Stop should-ing all over yourself

How did you come by your standards of perfection and how you define yourself? Or how many times do you say "I should" in one day? Some of these standards might be traced to your family of origin. Others might come from other seminal experiences, such as a summer spent with a grandparent or getting fired. As you can see from my Cambodia trip, these stories become so hardwired into how we see ourselves, it can take an unusual activity to jolt them to our awareness. Our goal is to help bring these stories to the surface and examine their usefulness in achieving our goals and making our life joyful.

This exercise was inspired by the book *The Trance of Scarcity* by Victoria Castle as well as the Newfield Coaching training. The core aspect of this exercise is to separate the facts from interpretation.[70] Once I examined the "should" of my story about being a warrior at all costs, I realized that I didn't need to keep killing myself on the bicycle to feel good about myself.

I realized that my old narrative—that my self-worth derived from being a competitive athlete—was too narrow and outdated. I realized that I was no longer defining myself as an athletic warrior. Once I accepted my new, broader view of myself, I was able to give myself permission to redefine myself and let go of a rigid and limiting standard.

Now it's your turn. This exercise works best if you answer the prompts in Step One on your own, then discuss Step Two with a trusted advisor or friend.

Step 1: Explore your "shoulds" or standards

Complete these sentences. Don't think too much; just write what comes to mind. Spend five to ten minutes and let all the shoulds out.

My parents should have done a better job of

_____

When I was young I should have

_____

Every day I should

_____

or I will become

_____

I should get involved in

_____

Otherwise I will

_____

I should always do

_____

To be more successful at work, I should

_____

At work, people should

_____

My boss should

_____

In my personal life, I should

_____

To stay in good physical shape, I should

_____

When on vacation, I should

_____

My spouse/partner should

_____

My children should

_____

The country should be

_____

What other things should you have done?

_____

_____

_____

_____

_____

What are your three most overwhelming or annoying "shoulds"?

1 _____

2 _____

3 _____

Step 2: Examine your "shoulds"

Select one or two of these "shoulds" that show up often and consistently, either bringing up negative emotions or holding you back.

Reflect on your three most annoying "shoulds" and start to reframe them and visualize the impact on your life. If you are struggling to reframe, begin with the potential impact. The goal is to stop mistaking our stories—or our shoulds—for the truth.

Read my reframing examples

Should	Reframe	Impact
Bike trip: Must ride all the time or you are wasting your money.	Biking is supposed to be fun—so only do it for as long as it is enjoyable; stop when it is not.	She enjoys the vacation.
Athletic warrior: I must always push myself. Otherwise, I am a wimp	My self-worth is not defined solely by my athletic prowess.	She chooses to bike when she wants, so it becomes fun.
Serious, work-focused woman: I must always be serious at work. Otherwise, I might be viewed as weak and less ambitious.	Not only can I show my warmth and sense of humor at work, doing that will help me connect more quickly and build a stronger network of support.	She forms broader relationships with more ease.
Working mother: I must do everything myself, both because no one can do it as well as I can, and because since I'm away from them a lot, I need to show them that I care. Otherwise, I am a not a good mother.	I can let go and delegate tasks that can be done more efficiently by others, such as cleaning the house. This will free me up to spend more quality, energizing time with my children and women friends.	She can take a Sunday off and have brunch and get massages with her women friends.

As you can see from my "shoulds," I've tended to have a rigid definition of performance and results. When I was a young competitive tennis player, the athletic warrior story had merit. But even though I mostly stopped playing serious competitive tennis in my late twenties and gave it up completely at thirty-five, I continued to define myself by these unrealistic benchmarks rather than adjust to the reality. Even worse, I was blaming myself for not being good enough, even though I am now in my fifties and only play tennis once or twice a week. Of course, I'm not going to perform like a twenty-something professional player who practices and plays for hours a day. Yet, I chastised myself internally because I wasn't pushing myself with my tennis or workouts—even though I no longer had the interest, and I was developing tendinitis in my shoulder.

Step 3: Create your new stories and reframe your shoulds

Brainstorm and explore three to five possible interpretations or stories that feel more energizing. It is fine to go crazy here and say outlandish and silly statements. Have some fun with it!

First, say the old should and then reframe out loud. Notice if—and how—your body feels differently as you tell each one.

I should

_____

_____

_____

Reframe with your new story

_____

_____

_____

Impact

_____

_____

_____

Reframe as many should as you'd like. Ask someone you trust to create a new story. I like asking someone I trust to create new stories or to select one for me, because they can be more objective.

Step 4: Moving forward

The final step is to select one new story that you want to adopt as a way to define yourself. Identify the positive ways this reframing could enhance your life. It's important to have a vision to go toward. Equally important, listen to your body.

Here are some questions to ask yourself as you decide which new reframe feels best. As with any of these exercises, while you can answer these questions on your own, the process can be easier and sometimes more insightful when done with a friend.

Unshackling questions:

- What about your old view feels heavy?

- What is holding you back or what are you afraid of?

- What is the worst thing that could happen if you adopt this view? Could you live with that?

New identity questions:

- What about the new reframe feels good?

- What or why is this new view so important? What do you really want/care about?

- What images and feelings arise when you think about the larger impact on your life?

- What is the tiniest step you can take or easiest win you can do right now? How does that feel?

The updated identity that I adopted on the bike trip instantly changed my behavior. I had a critical choice to make each day, which facilitated a swift letting go. But my self-definition around being a tennis player took much longer. The difference was that being a winning tennis player had become my identity at a young age. Perfectionists who started young, as I did, may benefit from additional professional therapy; these self-definitions are deeply entrenched.

I would encourage you to start with a goal at which you can have success. The working mother who hired a cleaner and started doing something fun once a month with her girlfriends found this small change made a huge positive impact. In her home life *and* at work, she stopped feeling so heavy and burdened.

If it does feel right, start saying it aloud at least once a day for the next thirty days. If it doesn't feel right, go back to reframing. The objective is to integrate this new story into your self-definition.

To continue to lighten the load, let's explore simple ways that we perfectionists can take ourselves a little less seriously.

Two minutes to your playful side

We are going to build upon letting go of your old heavy story and bring out your playful side. Bringing your playful side to work can help to build trust faster. And that's critical to productivity and innovation. Playfulness also encourages fearlessness and builds your skills around how to be flexible and adapt to change with more grace and ease.

Amy, the hard-nosed businesswoman who was mentioned earlier, learned the hard way. She discovered through the 360-degree interviews I conducted with her mostly male colleagues that they had trouble connecting with her because she was always so serious.

When I decided to stop playing competitive tennis in college due to performance anxiety, I started African dancing. This was my first entry into engaging in a physical activity at which I had zero talent and that I just did purely for fun and exercise. I was attracted to it because it was the opposite of tennis, comprised of freeing and playful movements. I was known in my African dancing class as the white Irish lady. With mirrors around the room, I couldn't help but notice how ungraceful and funny I looked as I flapped my arms or swayed from side to side or made leaps across the floor. The more I laughed at myself, the more I enjoyed the movements. No one judged me or ridiculed my spastic movements. Instead, I started to enjoy exercise again and found my sense of humor. African dancing was the beginning of a thirty-year journey of experimenting with different activities that helped me loosen up—even if I had no talent.

Similar to Amy Cuddy's Power Posing, discussed early on in the book, these activities could be completed in just a few minutes a day—or you could take longer when you have more time to play. Our focus here is to bring out your playful, silly, creative side. The two approaches are compatible. For instance, you can do Amy's Power Pose before engaging in African dancing, as a way to get outside of your comfort zone and into a playfulness that will make you happier and more flexible.

The idea is to select something that you either are curious about because it seems like fun or something at which you won't mind not excelling. One of the activities that has significantly lightened me up is improvisation, which I highly recommend to all self-proclaimed perfectionists.

My journey with improvisation

After college, I moved to New York City to begin my career in talent development/corporate HR work. I continued with therapy to help with my performance anxiety, which mostly showed up when I played competitive tennis. My therapist at the time suggested some new activities to loosen me up—improvisation and acting classes. Since I've always been a bit of a performer—first as a tennis player and now as a classroom trainer—I was intrigued. I loved watching "Saturday Night Live" and thought, "Why not? That looks like fun!"

I started taking basic improvisation classes at a local Jewish Community Center near my apartment. The class had about ten people of all ages. It began with simple warm-up exercises, in which we would have to pass along claps in a circle. One person would clap a certain way, turn, make eye contact, clap. The rest of us would imitate the clap and pass it along until the instructor would tell someone else to start a new movement to imitate, such as kicking a leg. The focus was on observation and listening. When, inevitably, someone made a mistake, we would laugh and applaud, saying, "I made a mistake!" The instructor was creating a safe and playful environment. Still, for a long time, it felt awkward for me; I would be self-critical every time I messed up, which was often.

There are many classic improvisation exercises. One of my favorites, which I've been using as a trainer and coach for thirty years, is "Yes, and". The purpose of this activity is to learn how to be open to the moment without judgment or thoughts. Since improvisation is a team exercise, each member must listen and communicate. It's also about learning to let go of your ego for the sake of the team.

For example, a common improvisation scene could be:

You go to the park to walk your dog, and you meet a strange-looking man who compliments you on your dog. If you ran away, as you might in real life, the scene would be over. So, in improvisation, you might say, "Yes, and thank you"—or get much deeper with something like, "Yes, and when I picked him out on my visit to Mars, the Martians were so excited that he would be returning to his native Earth!" In other words, you invite a response that allows the scene to continue.

"Yes, and" isn't about just repeating what the other person has said. It is about really saying yes with your mind and body to fully participating in the situation without trying to impress or be perfect. It is about just saying the first thing that comes to mind. The A-ha from this exercise is that the funniest comments come from listening and reacting in the moment.

There are two common mistakes. One, which I made for years, and many highly educated people make, is that instead of listening, you're already thinking tirelessly to come up with a clever answer. In the example, there might be a long pause or a long run-on sentence as you try to impress by explaining the dog's breeding heritage.

The second mistake is to say "Yes, but". Basically, you are saying no and asserting your ego. In the dog example, it might include an answer such as the dog is an extremely rare breed (explaining the details)—but please don't pet it.

It took me a couple of years to stop making these common mistakes. Finally, I started enjoying improvisation so much that I participated in the end-of-the-term performance that the class would do for a small group of invited guests.

Improvisation has transcended all aspects of my life. Mostly, it helped me trust myself in the moment. I know I can handle whatever people throw at me as a leader or a speaker. This allowed me to relax more and be a little lighter and more spontaneous. I remember speaking in front of a large audience many years later and my phone started ringing in my bag. I just walked over, turned it off, made a joke of it, and moved on. I realized I had moved beyond panicking. Like a true improvisor, I said "Yes, and" and used it to my advantage.

My enjoyment of improvisation led me to attend clown camp.

Why I went to clown camp and how it changed me

I was hired by Deloitte & Touche to lead their efforts to change the culture in the tri-state region from an accounting firm to a consultative/entrepreneurial culture. My boss, the head of HR and a former clown for Ringling Brothers, gave me feedback that I needed to lighten up if I wanted to be successful.

I was struggling with the challenge of getting accountants to be more consultative, creative, and engaging. I couldn't get past my observation that the accountants didn't seem open to change, which resulted in me starting to feel resigned and resentful.

As I reflected on my boss's feedback, I happened to meet a woman at a professional development event who ran a clown school in San Francisco. She convinced me that her clowning workshops could help me develop techniques for my work with the accountants. Again, I thought, "Why not?"

I learned there were two schools of clowning, American and European. My instructor taught the European method, which, I was relieved to learn, focused on developing a clown character, as opposed to actually wearing big, floppy red shoes and driving around in little cars.

A key exercise of the weekend was developing a clown walk that would be the basis of your clown's character. Like fashion models in Paris, we paraded across a runway while our fellow clowns observed and pointed out funny aspects of our walk. The aim was to identify something that was amusing about our walk, and then completely exaggerate it. Many of the others had a single glaring flaw like big hips or a limp, which in this class worked to their advantage. I am tall and thin—nothing funny going on here. Worse yet, just weeks before I had completed the Alexander Technique, a postural education process. So, I now had an otherwise-enviable classic walk. This made the clown-walk exercise a very humbling experience. It showed that my now-perfect posture was boring. Luckily, I tripped at the end of the walk. And that became my character—the perfect walker with an occasional stumble.

My clown character's name was Sassy. Sassy wore clothing that was too small and exaggerated her tall, skinny frame. She also wore a little hat and a red nose. The rest of the weekend was spent attempting to juggle—failed at it miserably—and working with props like little purses to go with my outfit. By the end of the weekend, I was feeling very imperfect and maybe even a little funny.

Returning to reality after clowning was enlightening. As a tall, willowy blonde woman working with accountants who are stereotypically quiet, nebbish men, mostly on the short side, I realized that maybe I wasn't necessarily any more amusing or interesting than any of them. I was seeing the world differently now.

I went into the workshop thinking that I would learn techniques to help accountants adopt new behaviors. But I realized that *I* might be the one who needed to change if I wanted to be more effective in working with *them*.

Clowning taught me that it's those little, imperfect, and intrinsically human things that make people interesting. I came back humbled, more creative, and most importantly, more accepting. And who knows—maybe even a little funnier. I started focusing on getting to know the people I was working with—to find ways to connect, rather than to judge.

As you can see, the performing arts have a lot to offer us perfectionists. For me, they've taken me out of my negative self-talk and heaviness and brought me more lightness. I've recommended these types of programs to many of my coaching clients, who have also found them helpful.

I want to share the list of what has helped me, and others lighten up.

Playful activities that I've tried (and you might want to):
Hula-Hooping

Improvisation classes

Acting classes

Drawing

Painting

Creative writing

Clown school

Cooking

Rollerblading

Journey dancing (a style of free form dancing and self-reflection)

Belly dancing

Dancing with your children in front of the TV for five minutes

Jamming to your favorite music for two minutes between meetings

Non-impact aerobic dancing

Beer tasting and making

Going to the gym

Guilty pleasures such as window-shopping at an expensive store

Coloring in an adult coloring book for ten minutes

As you can see, there are a lot of artistic activities on the list. I'd always thought of myself as creative but lacking artistic talent. I had always wanted to try drawing and painting, just for fun. I found out I have limited artistic talent, but that painting can be quite calming. My journey has been humbling and enlightening; I've realized my talent limitations while being energized by learning new activities. The biggest challenge has been to let go of negative judgments about my performance.

Many of the activities on this list require time and money, while some, such as Hula-Hooping or dancing, do not. The end goal is to find a way to integrate these activities into your life. One easy way to start is to purchase and use an adult coloring book; they've become very popular. You can come home from work and color for five minutes to end the stress of the day and rejuvenate.

Exercises—becoming lighter without going on a diet

These exercises are meant for busy, conscientious types who tend to take themselves too seriously. Lightening up is going to take some practice—and we perfectionists excel at practice. The potential benefits are huge. These activities can lead to a more solid sense of self, expanded sense of humor and lightness about yourself, and re-energized productivity.

Identify activities that you are curious about or think might be enjoyable. Is there a skill, sport, or activity that you think would be fun? Remember, the aim is not to become skilled, just to loosen you up. You've seen my list, so you already know there are no limits here except your imagination. There are two ways you can approach this exercise: You can add something easy to your repertoire that can be done every day, or you can take a longer workshop. Spend five to seven minutes and list as many activities as possible. Don't edit or limit yourself.

Review the list and identify two types of activities:

- Those that you can do for five minutes a day, such as Hula-Hooping or dancing to your favorite artist.

- Those that require more of an investment, such as taking an improvisation class or starting a new sport such as rollerblading.

Hula-Hooping has become a staple in my new lighten-up diet

As I shared in an earlier chapter, once I discovered that the secret to Hula-Hooping as an adult is having the right hoop, it became my favorite way to celebrate a Situational Win. It's also my favorite playful activity. I now Hula-Hoop for three to five minutes at least three days a week. I find Hula-Hooping makes me feel silly and childlike, which is the antidote for my serious perfectionist self. As more people work from home, a simple activity like Hula-Hooping can be added to your day. I'm always amazed at how three minutes of Hula-Hooping can change my mood from anxious or overwhelmed to light and relaxed, which in turn makes me more productive.

How busy working women weave in playfulness

Let me share some other simple examples of how working women are finding ways to insert playfulness into their busy schedules.

When I discussed this idea of a playful activity such as Hula-Hooping with one of my previous coaching clients, Christine, she laughed. Christine realized that she didn't really have a hobby outside of work other than hanging out with family and friends. She is a nursing executive who works long hours and is very dedicated to her job. After thinking about it, Christine decided that she literally needed to loosen up by adding a neck and back massage to her weekly manicure. This was a huge deal for her. As Christine started doing this on a regular basis, she became a bit lighter and more compassionate towards herself and others.

In contrast, when I brought the idea of a playful activity up with a lawyer, Sally, who works in finance, she loved it. She's a working mother with two young children, and she felt that she didn't have enough fun in her life. As she was working on her list, she realized that she loves to dance and hang out with her children. So, she married the two by having brief nightly dancing parties with her kids. They would select their favorite music and dance wildly in the living room. As she danced at least once a week with her children, she started to lighten up at work, which helped her manage a challenging situation by being more relaxed and calmer.

Lastly, another client, Joan, a lawyer who worked in finance, hit her mid-forties and felt like she was going through her mid-life crisis. Joan felt bored and uninspired at work. She felt she should spend whatever free time she had with her five-year-old daughter. As we examined her shoulds, she realized that if she could do something fun or energizing for herself, she would be a better mother. She loves to write and felt she had stories in her that she wanted to share with the world. She signed up for an online fiction writing course and is now writing for thirty minutes a few days a week. She still struggles with working-mother guilt but is enjoying the writing and feeling happier overall.

Wrap-up

As you can see from these stories, there are many ways to lighten up—and the benefits can be far-reaching. The challenge for us perfectionists is that we take ourselves very seriously. We get things done, and that's important. But those may not be the things that help us take our careers forward or build stronger connections with key colleagues. Over and over again, I observe that when we spend even small amounts of time engaged in playful activities that give us joy, we're more likely to be productive, innovative, and effective at our current jobs—or more likely to make a change to do something that makes us happier and ultimately more successful.

This was the case with Sally, the lawyer who worked in finance. As she became happier, she decided she could no longer work at her current company. She gave notice, and within the next six months started winding down her current role and looking for a new job in an organization that would be a better fit.

Sally's story shows it's more productive for everyone when we work in situations that energize us. Wouldn't you rather work in a world where people are engaged and charged up about their roles? Similarly, Joan's enjoyment of her creative writing course encouraged her to find ways to use those skills in her writing as a lawyer, which in turn gave her more job satisfaction.

Shackle-smashing actions

The focus is on how to build new sensations in the body that make you feel lighter and more positive, which in turn create new perspectives and, in turn, more possibilities. The goal is to keep asking yourself, "Does this action make me feel tight, heavy, and constrained—and if so, what small step can melt those shackles?"

Here are a couple of examples.

What's one small step you can take to break out of your shackles?

Start your day by saying your reframed should to yourself. One of my favorites is, "I will do what is most important on my to-do list and let go and reprioritize the rest without guilt."

If you don't know what your shoulds are, start making a list. Get a small notebook and write down one should per day or week. What do you notice?

Share an annoying should with a friend and ask him/her to reframe it.

What's one small physical action you can take to break out of your shackles?

- My go-to approach is to notice when I feel tight and heavy.

Take five deep belly breaths to calm down. Make these breaths long and slow, counting to four as you breathe in and out. I do this simple exercise on the subway, in the restroom, or walking to a meeting. It always helps me relax and focus.

- My other favorite exercise is to play a much-loved song in between meetings and dance—when I'm in a place where I can.

- Buy a big Hula-Hoop and practice for two to three minutes a day, preferably to your favorite music. If you didn't buy my Hula-Hoop with this book, there's still time; they are available on my website. I try to Hula-Hoop whenever I am working at home all day as a reward for completing a task.

CHAPTER 11

How to Manage a Perfectionists: Bosses, Colleagues, and Direct Reports

"Take criticism seriously, but not personally. If there is truth or merit in the criticism, try to learn from it. Otherwise, let it roll right off you."

Hilary Rodham Clinton, First Lady, Senator, and Secretary of State, *Living History*, 2003

We've covered a lot of ground in this book. Now we'll put the tools together to solve real-world challenges. One of the most commonly asked questions in my Productive Perfectionist workshops is, "How do I work with a boss who is a perfectionist?" How do I figure out if my potential employer has a perfectionist culture?

Many people work in cultures that reward people who don't ask questions and just put their heads down and work longer and harder than everyone else. How do you navigate these challenging situations?

This chapter will include suggested steps using all the techniques in the book and refer you back to earlier discussed scenarios. Remember, the only person you can change is yourself—and the best result might only make the person less annoying. It may not be the perfect ending, but it will be acceptable.

Five common perfectionist challenges:

- How to work with a demanding/difficult boss.

- How to manage an overachieving direct report.

- How to manage a difficult/challenging colleague or client.

- How to survive an unfriendly or hostile work environment.

- How to figure out before you start a new job if the culture is perfectionist—questions to ask in the interview process.

The approach

These approaches mirror the five actions of productive perfectionists, discussed earlier in the chapter on how perfectionism is limiting (with slight variations). I will present the tips and refer back to an example of each. We'll start with what I think are the easiest and then move to the more difficult. You'll notice that the action tips overlap across categories. That's because the basic principles are true in any interaction with a person you find challenging. But because each situation is a little different, some of the steps are different in each category.

Three steps to managing that challenging colleague or client

This could be a colleague/client who is annoying and challenging for any number of reasons, from micromanaging every detail to overwhelming need for inclusion.

- Assume innocence, have compassion, and attempt to stay light.

- Understand what you need and want from this colleague/client to be successful. What is your Situational Win?

- Observe this colleague/client and notice what motivates him or her. Identify the degree they are energized by the following areas, based on the FIRO-B that we discussed in chapter seven.[71]

Do they have high or low needs for the following:

- **Inclusion.** Want to be involved in group meetings and want recognition from others; high-needs people want to be included in everything from the holiday party to important work events—and titles matter—whereas those with low needs are more selective and don't want recognition unless it is deserved.

- **Control.** Need to take charge and be involved in every decision and detail; high-needs people want to be leading and engaged in the big picture and in the details, while low-needs tend to be independent, flexible, and selective regarding where they need to be in control.

- **Affection.** Desire friendly and open one-on-one relation-ships with people at work; high needs don't distinguish between work and personal friends and always share details about their personal lives, whereas those with low needs tend to keep work and personal relationships separate.

Make consistent deposits that relate to a core need for a challenging colleague/client. For example, those with high needs for inclusion want to be invited to all group meetings and be publicly recognized, whereas those with low needs only want to be included in group events that directly relate to their interests. Those with high needs need more frequent attention, whereas those with lower needs require more selective attention that relates to their interests.

Ask for feedback regarding how things are going. It is helpful, especially with new relationships to ask if people are feeling included. Are they receiving information that is adding to their day or does it feel overwhelming or draining?

Refer to Fiona's story (see page 139) where she learned how to manage Jill through adapting to her top needs based on the FIRO-B. Fiona's example shows how she made consistent deposits to Jill's top needs.

Refer to Dina's story (see page 88) where she had to manage rela-tionships with crucial male traders who were challenging her every move. She focused on making deposits to their inclusion needs.

Refer to Amy's story (see page 169) where she learned to use lightness and humor to build relationships with her main male colleagues.

Five steps to managing the perfectionist/difficult manager

One of the most common reasons people leave jobs is because of a difficult boss. Before you quit—or start smoking again—let's explore some small steps:

- Assume innocence, have compassion, and attempt to stay light.

- Ask your manager the five key questions on his definition of success (see pages 141–142); your goal is to determine how to reduce the tension in the relationship. If they offer a lot of negative feedback, continue to calmly inquire how the feedback links to expectations and ask for specifics on what better performance would look like.

- Make consistent deposits that harness their definition of success to create a positive emotional bank account.

- Observe and ask for feedback regarding what deposits generate the most positive responses and what pet peeves seem to annoy the most.

- Identify and accept the Situational Win for the relationship. What can you live with?

Refer to the Fiona and Jill story (see page 139), where Fiona had to adapt her style to the style of her new manager, who had much lower needs for inclusion and affection.

Refer to Sara's story (see page 54) on how she learned to use self-compassion and humor to manage a boss who did not want to retire.

Five steps to managing the high-achieving direct report

While it might seem like a dream to have someone on your team who wants to do everything to a very high standard and never says no, it's not sustainable in the long run. Here are some tips to help the person break out of those tendencies:

- Assume innocence, have compassion, and attempt to stay light.

- Ask questions to learn whether they're motivated more by direct or less direct feedback. Do they want you to tell them head on that they are making mistakes—or do they want some sugar on top?

- Share your expectations of success regarding the person's work/working relationship, get their agreement, and hold them accountable.

- Follow the three-to-one rule for feedback: Provide three positive pieces of feedback/deposits to their emotional bank account for every constructive suggestion.

- Observe how they react to your feedback, ask how things are going, and adjust accordingly.

Lessons learned from managing a perfectionist

When I was running a global talent management department, I had five direct reports based in New York, London, and Hong Kong. I would hold regular staff meetings and one-on-ones. One of my top performers was based in New York. She always did excellent work and desperately wanted a promotion to vice president. I was supportive of it, but I didn't realize at the time that she was practically killing herself to make it happen. She would never say no and would volunteer for many projects. She would never complain when I asked her if she was overwhelmed.

I worked until eight or nine at night on occasion a few times a month. When I was in the midst of a large project, we worked together until eight or later every night, every week. The week after we completed the project, I worked until nine one evening in the office, and I found her there again. I asked to speak to her the next day and inquired into how often this was occurring. She said, "Almost every day."

I was stunned. I instantly realized I had not asked her enough questions and made clear that working regularly until nine was not a sustainable strategy. After a lengthy conversation, we shifted some deadlines and responsibilities and her work/life balance improved. She shared how much she enjoyed working with me on that project and asked if we could work together more often. I changed my behavior to ask more questions, include her on projects when possible, and drop by more often. Our relationship *and* the results both improved.

How to survive an unfriendly or hostile work environment

You might find yourself in a work environment that seems unfriendly or in which you feel like a minority. If you want to stay at this job and make it workable, try these steps. Sometimes just stepping back and taking better care of yourself and asserting your needs can help. At some point, the best option might still be to leave—but these steps will make sure you have given the job a fair chance.

- Focus on finding self-compassion and adopt a positive affirmation that you say regularly, especially before difficult meetings.

- Identify what makes you happy in life. What do you want from this job? What's a possible Situational Win? Do you need to attend one of your child's recreational events? Do you want to drop your child off at school?

- Ask your manager about his or her expectations of you and the five key questions regarding how they work (see page 141) so you can make sure you are on the same page. And if the manager gives a lot of criticism, ask questions about how this relates to his/her expectations of you and what specifically you can do to improve. Write this down and check in periodically to see if things are improving.

- Make consistent deposits that relate to one of your manager's core needs and to their emotional bank account. For example, ask about their weekend or compliment them on an accomplishment. Then request something important to you, such as taking a half-day off to attend your daughter's dance recital. Periodically check in and ask for feedback regarding how things are going and adjust. In addition, make deposits with key colleagues to create a more supportive network. Spend time with people who are supportive.

- Make sure to increase the self-care and activities that bring you joy. This will help to counter the effects of a toxic environment.

Refer to the story of Faye (see page 29). She is a self-proclaimed perfectionist and single working mother who worked in a male-dominated industry and found a way to get beyond survival—to thrive.

Refer to my story in Failure as a Badge of Honor on how I survived and bounced back from a failure.

Questions to ask during the interview process to determine if the culture is perfectionist:

We all want to work in a meritocracy, where we are judged fairly for the work we do and allowed to bring our best self to work. Unfortunately, this is very difficult to create and maintain. No place is going to get it all right. What's important is to ask questions that help you understand what is valued and rewarded—and to ask these questions in a way that forces the interviewee to share real world examples versus the company line:

- Tell me about how the year-end/feedback/compensation process works.

- How often is performance feedback given? Can you provide common examples, such as at the end of projects or at mid-year and year-end?

- What type of employee succeeds and does well? What are the qualities that are valued?

- Give me an example of why someone would get promoted.

- How have you managed your career at the company? What can hold you back?

- What are the typical hours/work weeks?

- What type of management/leadership training and coaching is provided? What levels and who attends these? Is it mandatory? Why or why not?

These questions are meant to help you understand how much the organization values creating a culture that provides regular positive and constructive feedback, clear guidelines around promotions, reasonable work hours, and the training of managers and leaders. What you are looking for is transparency around these company processes and their values around building a workplace that actually seems to care about people, versus achieving results at all costs.

CHAPTER 12

Wrap-up: How to Stay Inspired and Inspire Future Generations

"When the whole world is silent, even one voice becomes powerful."

Malala Yousafzai, education activist, Harvard Foundation Peter Gomes Award acceptance speech, September 27, 2013

I f women want to make an impact in the world, we need to jump in, even when we're not quite prepared.

As of January 2019, one hundred and thirty-one women served in the United States Congress—the most ever. This group of women represents many firsts: The first women representing their states; the first Native American women, and the first Muslim women in all of Congress; the first openly gay senator, and so on.

Many of these women decided to run with little to no experience in politics—and often, with little or no precedent in their states for women getting elected. As I read about their stories in a special *The New York Times* article, I was deeply inspired. For example, Elissa Slotkin, a freshman Democrat from Michigan, was inspired to run after seeing her representative from Michigan vote to repeal the Affordable Health Care Act. This was personal to her after watching her mother die in 2011 of ovarian cancer and struggling to receive healthcare due to Elissa's own pre-existing condition.[72]

In today's fast-moving world, risk-taking is required, not optional. Most organizations are flatter, less hierarchical, and more team-oriented than ten to twenty years ago. The largest generation in the workplace now is the Millennials, who want to follow their passions and do work they love. The average tenure at a job for these Millennials is less than three years.[73] If you want to retain Millennials and make them productive, they need to feel connected to the mission/vision of the organization; they need to be inspired.

Therein lies the rub: Most perfectionists are inspired by hard work. I know that for me, it was about trudging forward with a fist in the back. Get in early, stay late, take ten minutes to shove down a sandwich at your desk, and just outwork everyone—that should be inspiring!

How not to inspire

Stevie, a fifty-three-year-old senior managing director at a small global financial services firm that focuses on managing pensions, was struggling to inspire her large team full of Millennials. She felt that she'd lost her mojo and wanted it back. So, she hired me as her coach. She grew up in the produce-or-die investment banking and consulting industries for decades and chose to come to this smaller firm because it was friendlier and moved at a slightly slower pace. She wanted to enjoy time with her family rather than working eighty-plus hours a week. But she still wanted to achieve big things and felt like she and her team were not on the same page.

Stevie had been working sixty-plus-hour weeks, always the first in and the last to leave. Constantly on airplanes, doing whatever it took to win business and succeed. But Stevie was getting tired and frustrated—and wondering why her team was running out the door at 5:01 every night while she toiled away until seven. When I asked her about the situation, Stevie said she'd assumed that hard work should be an inspiration—but that obviously it wasn't working. When I asked her what inspired her, she realized she didn't know.

In thinking about this, I remembered an experience of my own when I became burned out from competitive tennis. I became a good player because I was passionate about the sport. Twenty years later, I wasn't enjoying the sport any longer. Tennis had become my identity, and I felt like I was only playing because I didn't know what else to do. It took a breather from the competition to get back in touch with the simple joys of hitting a tennis ball. How could I help Stevie get back in touch with her passion?

Go on a sensation hunt

I took my inspiration from an experience of my own. It was a snowy day in the Catskills—a rarity these days. I started to panic. I didn't know how to ski on fresh powder—only groomed snow or East Coast ice. Luckily, I was attending Mermer Blakslee's Fear Clinic. Mermer is an expert on fear and the author of one of my favorite books, *A Conversation with Fear*.[74] I'd been attending her clinic for several years.

Mermer encouraged us to play with sensation hunts. Instead of thinking, "I want to ski on groomed trails," try to feel the snow under your skis. Notice how the snow feels: the softness, the bumps, and the fluffiness of the flakes. Surrender to the moment and let go of control. As a perfectionist, letting go is one of the most difficult things. But I soon realized that panicking was not helping me ski better. I stopped and took a breath, felt compassion for myself as I acknowledged my fear and lack of experience or comfort skiing in fresh snow.

As a Driven to Succeed person, I enjoy doing things well better than proving that I can ski in snowy conditions. Once I accepted that I may not do this well, I started to relax and enjoy the moment. I slowed down, took my time, looked around at the white blanket all around me, and attempted to just listen and feel the snow.

I even started acting like a ten-year-old child, sticking out my tongue and catching snowflakes. My skiing isn't pretty, but I realized that I have more ability than I give myself credit for. I can ski in these conditions if I stay in the moment and keep noticing and feeling compassion and joy.

Since my playful sensation hunt calmed me down and lightened me up to find my ski legs and enjoy the moment, I decided to ask Stevie to do a work-related version.

Go on an inspiration hunt

To see if I could slow her down and bring her into the present, I asked Stevie to go on an inspiration hunt—to reflect on the question: What enlivens you? Small things count: a random act of kindness, a delicious dinner, a heartwarming story.

Stevie's A-ha moment was similar to mine as I panicked on the snow. She realized that she's inspired by aiming big—by excellence. A former college athlete, she enjoyed striving to improve and keep improving. She understood that she had become resigned and had given up on herself. She was now aiming for mediocrity. She was getting annoyed frequently and needed to refocus herself.

I noticed that Stevie talked fast and rarely smiled. We did a brief, deep-breathing exercise. I asked her to sit up in her chair, get comfortable, close her eyes, take five slow deep breaths, and just see how this felt. This helped her slow down and center herself. She started practicing this regularly.

To let go of control and allow yourself to be present is no small step for a perfectionist. This led Stevie to realize that she needed more exercise. Instead of calling into meetings, she started walking to and from meetings in another office, which helped her feel more energized.

Get your mojo back

We continued to discuss what aiming for excellence might look like. What small steps could she take?

Stevie shared that when she and a small team had pitched business to the CEO of a potential new client, two out of the four young members on her team had showed up to meet the CEO with khakis and brown shoes, no tie or jacket. Stevie, who believes that a core part of striving for excellence means dressing the part, was horrified. Having been brought up in investment banking and consulting, Stevie usually wore a jacket or a suit to work even though the dress code had become business casual a couple of years ago. She didn't like the new dress code; it felt too laissez-faire.

When they didn't win the business, she saw her opportunity. She created a story about how much she cares about wanting to strive for excellence and her real belief in her team. Stevie's small financial services company regularly competes against much bigger competitors. This means that every little detail matters. The winning team in the recent pitch all came dressed in suits. It certainly wasn't the only reason they lost the business. But if a CEO is going to hire them to manage their millions of dollars of pension money, her team needs to win their trust.

She wanted the speech to be inspiring. So, we practiced.

The trickiest part of delivering the message was to get into the right mood—ambition, not resignation. She needed to show her warmth and vulnerability.

Research shows that if you focus first on demonstrating support for and belief in the team and only secondarily on competence and the organization's ability to deliver results for clients, people will not only comply outwardly, they'll be much more likely to adopt the values and bigger mission that Stevie was aiming toward. [75]

This was a huge shift for Stevie. In the past, she'd focused on what went wrong and telling everyone to step up. And she'd gotten only short-term compliance without buy-in. Once Stevie got in touch with her care, she was able to show warmth via a sincere smile, speak in a tone that showed she was leveling with people, and share that she, too, was frustrated with recent losses and wanted to win more often. Stevie shared how she felt at the last pitch when their competitors all came in suits and her team came half in suits and half in khakis. She'd felt disappointed that the team's appearance didn't match its capabilities. Stevie wanted to win pitches like this and asked if others also wanted to win. Would they be willing to dress the part to increase their odds that they might win more deals? This led to more of the team expressing their agreement with and support of her larger vision and small request.

Small steps can lead to big results. That is the journey of the productive perfectionist. If you don't know what to do next, sit and take five deep breaths—even on the subway, or at your desk. Spend five minutes writing down ten things you are grateful for. Go for a walk. Or try my favorite activity: two minutes of listening to happy music while twirling my pink Hula-Hoop. For me, it always leads to a more productive day.

Embrace your inner productive perfectionist

Given that we perfectionists love to check things off our lists, let's return to the five actions. Let's see if you feel more comfortable getting out of your comfort zone.

These five actions disrupt the fist-in-the-back approach, build lighter and more expansive new possibilities and sensations in the body, and eventually override the tight, heavy, and constrained feelings of perfectionism. You've probably made progress in some areas while in others, you might have slid back to old ways.

Five actions of productive perfectionists

- **Build a positive emotional foundation.** Clarify the ways that three positive emotions—joy, gratitude, and compassion—can keep perfectionism from overwhelming you and learn the daily practices that result in increased productivity.

- **Strive for the Situational Win: excellence instead of perfection.** Set your definitions of accomplishment within each specific situation, both for yourself and for your team. This approach helps you make progress on your goals, adapt quickly to change, and enjoy your life overall.

- **Learn how to evaluate what risks to take—and how to rebound safely from slip-ups.** Understand your approach to getting out of your comfort zone; take steps to make risk-taking simpler and rebounding faster.

- **Create a safety net of trusted relationships.** Learn to be vulnerable in select ways, such as asking for help and giving credit, so you can build trust more quickly and increase your comfort with risk-taking.

- **Lighten up! Get rid of limiting shoulds,** such as, "I should have a clean house," and instead create empowering new mantras, such as, "I can hire a housecleaner and accept that my house will be clean enough." Identify activities that encourage playfulness. It could be Hula-Hooping five minutes a day, taking a singing course, or any other passion that brings joy outside of work achievements—and results in more creativity, innovation, and productivity.

Productive perfectionism self-assessment: examine your comfort with the five actions

Becoming self-aware is the foundation for working and living more productively. Now that you've gone through the book, it's time to retake the Productive Perfectionist Self-assessment.

Note where you were when you started on the scale between unproductive and productive perfectionist. Remember the purpose of the productive perfectionist is to be able to do things well, take risks, rebound quickly, manage the expectations/demands of others, and enjoy the process.

Here are a few steps to consider:
- Identify areas in which you already feel comfortable practicing and those that you want to enhance. Where have you made progress? Remember the results do not measure skill but frequency and comfort.

- What actions need increased practice to become a habit? Start small and select one that could generate the most value for you in your life. The key is to identify the strengths you can build upon and those one to two areas that you could benefit from performing more often.

Congratulations on reading the entire book! Given that we perfectionists are busy and thrive on the challenge to do things well. I challenge you to find at least five minutes every day to be kinder to yourself and look for ways that you can bring your full value to the world. The world needs the conscientiousness and care that perfectionists have to offer. Until we take care of ourselves, the world can't receive the full benefit of our contributions.

The favorite productive perfectionist actions

Here are some of the core actions that I have found perfectionists tend to gain the most from adding to their repertoire and a few others:

- Take five deep breaths.

- Take five minutes to write down a gratitude list or say it to yourself as you take a walk to the train or to and from your office.

- Start a value-add list of your key contributions; spend five minutes adding to it every week.

- When you start working with someone and/or take on a new project, take time to ask "What would excellence look like? What is good enough?" Get clear agreements.

- Periodically analyze your mistakes. Write about it or talk with a friend and ask yourself: What are the situational factors that led to your decision? What are the universal qualities that are good about you? What would you do differently next time? Then let it go.

- Write a bold declaration for something you really want in your life. Example: I want to help the next generation of women rise up and take bold risks!

- Determine if you are Driven to Prove or Driven to Succeed. Develop a plan to expand your comfort zone to stretch and rebound faster. And, if you're really feeling brave, find someone to mentor you who has a different approach.

- Look for small ways to support other people's dreams, such as making introductions or writing a positive recommendation to their boss or on LinkedIn.

- Make a small request of someone you trust. It could be to listen to you share a current challenging situation—or what you want to do this weekend.

- Ask for feedback from someone you trust. What went well? What is one thing I could have done to make it better?

- List your shoulds in five minutes. Pick the most annoying one and ask a friend to reframe. Experiment with saying the new declaration aloud. How does it make you feel?

- Make time to celebrate the small victories with activities you find fun and rewarding—such as Hula-Hooping for five minutes after finishing a difficult task or spending a half day at a spa with friends when you clinch a terrific deal.

These are just a few ideas. What are your favorites?

If you choose to start taking five minutes for breathing, asking more questions, and for feedback, you'll notice that you start to feel lighter, less isolated. Becoming a productive perfectionist is about creating a life that will bring out the best in you without feeling that you must constantly be accomplishing to feel good about yourself. It may feel counterintuitive—but the more you practice these tiny steps, the more you will start to believe and before you know it, you will be working differently.

When you start embodying this new way of living, you may inspire others to join. Wouldn't it be nice to imagine a world in which women aren't holding themselves back by striving for unrealistic expectations? Rather, women are using their talents and strengths to create a world that helps everyone play their biggest game.

BIBLIOGRAPHY

Allen, David. *Getting Things Done: The Art of Stress-Free Productivity*. New York: Penguin, 2001.

Beck, Martha. *The Joy Diet: 10 Daily Practices for a Happier Life*. New York: Harmony, 2003.

Blakeslee, Mermer. *A Conversation with Fear*. CreateSpace Independent Publishing Platform, 2016.

Brown, Brené. *Daring Greatly: How the Courage to Be Vulnerable Transforms the Way We Live, Love, Parent, and Lead*. New York: Penguin Group, 2012.

Castle, Victoria. *The Trance of Scarcity: Stop Holding Your Breath and Start Living Your Life*. Oakland: Berrett-Koehler, 2007.

Childre, Doc, and Howard Martin. *The Heartmath Solution*. San Francisco: Harper One, 1999.

Covey, Stephen R. *The 7 Habits of Highly Effective People*. New York: Free Press, 2004.

Cross, Rob, and Robert J. Thomas. *Driving Results Through Social Networks: How Top Organizations Leverage Networks for Performance and Growth*. San Francisco: Jossey-Bass, 2008.

Cuddy, Amy. *Presence: Bringing Your Boldest Self to Your Biggest Challenges*. Boston: Little Brown and Company, 2015.

DeLuca, Joel R. *Political Savvy: Systematic Approaches to Leadership Behind the Scenes*. Berwyn, PA; Evergreen Business Group, 1999.

Dotlich, David L., and Peter C. Cairo. *Why CEOs Fail: The 11 Behaviors That Can Derail Your Climb to the Top and How to Manage Them*. New York: Wiley, 2003.

Dweck, Carol. *Mindset: The New Psychology of Success*. New York: Random House, 2006.

Goleman, Daniel. *Emotional Intelligence (EQ): Why It Can Matter More Than IQ*. New York: Bantam, 1995.

Grant, Adam. *Give and Take: Why Helping Others Drives Our Success*. New York: Viking, 2013.

Grant, Adam. *Originals: How Non-Conformists Move the World*. New York: Viking, 2016.

Hewlett, Sylvia Ann. *Forget a Mentor, Find a Sponsor: The New Way to Fast-Track Your Career*. Brighton, MA: Harvard Business Review Press, 2013.

Kay, Katty, and Claire Shipman. *The Confidence Code: The Science and Art of Self-Assurance—What Women Should Know*. New York: Harper Business, 2018.

Lamott, Anne. *Bird by Bird: Some Instructions on Writing and Life*. New York: Pantheon Books, 1994.

Loehr, James E. *Stress for Success*. New York: Three Rivers Press, 1997.

Maurer, Robert. *One Small Step Can Change Your Life: The Kaizen Way*. New York: Workman, 2004.

Mayer, Kathryn C. *Collaborative Competition: A Woman's Guide to Succeeding by Competing*. Collaborative Competition Press, 2009.

Moore, Geoffrey A. *Crossing the Chasm: Marketing and Selling Disruptive Products to Mainstream Customers*. New York: Harper Business, 1994.

Musselwhite, Ed. FIRO-B: *Interpersonal Dimensions: Understanding Your FIRO-B Results*. Washington, DC: Consulting Psychologists Press, 1982.

Rubin, Gretchen. *The Happiness Project: Or, Why I Spent a Year Trying to Sing in the Morning, Clean My Closets, Fight Right, Read Aristotle, and Generally Have More Fun*. New York: HarperCollins, 2009.

Sandberg, Sheryl. *Lean In: Women, Work, and the Will to Lead*. New York: Knopf, 2013.

Spar, Debora L. *Wonder Women: Sex, Power, and the Quest for Perfection*. London: Picador, 2014.

Tschannen-Moran, Megan. *Trust Matters: Leadership for Successful Schools*. San Francisco: Jossey-Bass, 2004.

Waterman, Judith A., and Jenny Rogers. *Introduction to the FIRO-B Instrument*. Washington, DC: Consulting Psychologists Press, 1996.

Young, Valerie. *The Secret Thoughts of Successful Women: Why Capable People Suffer from the Impostor Syndrome and How to Thrive in Spite of It*. New York: Crown Business, 2011.

ENDNOTES

1   Anne Lamott, *Bird by Bird* (New York: Pantheon Books, 1994), page 27.

2   Adam Grant, *Originals* (New York: Viking, 2016), pages 37–38.

3   Adam Davidson, "Welcome to the Failure Age!," *New York Times Magazine*, November 12, 2014.

4   Marcus Noland and Tyler Moran, "Study: Firms with More Women in the C-Suite Are More Profitable," *Harvard Business Review*, February 08, 2016, https://hbr.org/2016/02/study-firms-with-more-women-in-the-c-suite-are-more-profitable/.

5   Jennifer Openshaw, cited in "The Number 1 Reason Women Don't Get Promoted At Work" by Ruchika Tulshyan, https://www.forbes.com/sites/ruchikatulshyan/2015/02/19/the-number-1-reason-women-dont-get-promoted-at-work/?sh=1c802d225d9c

6   Katty Kay and Claire Shipman, *The Confidence Code* (New York: Harper Business, 2018), pages 133–145.

7   David L. Dotlich and Peter C. Cairo, *Why CEOs Fail* (New York: Wiley, 2003), pages 116–126.

8   Carol Dweck, *Mindset* (New York: Random House, 2006), pages 6–7.

9   Mackenzie Erin Beltz, "Cindy Sherman," *Contemporary Art or Why "I Could've Done That" Is Irrelevant*, September 26, 2014, https://sites.psu.edu/mbeltzpassionblog/2014/09/26/cindy-sherman/#more-20/.

10   Daniel Goleman, *Emotional Intelligence* (EQ) (New York: Bantam, 1995), pages 33–45.

11   Doc Childre and Howard Martin, *The HeartMath Solution* (San Francisco: Harper One, 1999), pages 3–23.

12   Amy Cuddy, *Presence* (Boston: Little Brown and Company, 2015), pages 174–180.

13   Amy Cuddy, *Presence*; and Amy Cuddy, "Your Body Language May Shape Who You Are," *TEDGlobal 2012*, 20:46, https://www.ted.com/talks/amy_cuddy_your_body_language_may_shape_who_you_are/c/.

14   Pauline R. Clance and Suzanne A. Imes, "The Impostor Phenomenon in High Achieving Women: Dynamics and Therapeutic Intervention," *Psychotherapy: Theory, Research & Practice* 15, no. 3 (Fall 1978): pages 241–247.

15   L.V. Anderson, "Feeling Like an Imposter Is Not a Syndrome," *Slate*, April 12, 2016, https://slate.com/business/2016/04/is-impostor-syndrome-real-and-does-it-affect-women-more-than-men.html/.

16   Valerie Young, *The Secret Thoughts of Successful Women* (New York: Crown Business, 2011), pages 1–11.

17   Joseph Cesario, Kai J. Jonas, and Dana R. Caney, "CRSP Special Issue on Power Poses: What Was the Point and What Did We Learn?," *Comprehensive Results in Social Psychology*, June 28, 2017, https://doi.org/10.1080/23743603.2017.1309876; Eva Ranehill et al., "Assessing the Robustness of Power Posing: No Effect on Hormones and Risk Tolerance in a Large Sample of Men and Women," *Psychological Science* 26, no. 5 (2015): https://doi.org/10.1177/0956797614553946; Dana Carney, "'My Position on 'Power Poses'": faculty.haas.berkeley.edu/dana_carney/pdf_My%20position%20on%20power%20poses.pdf.

18   Robert Maurer, *One Small Step Can Change Your Life* (New York: Workman, 2004), pages 39–48.

19   Amy Cuddy, *Presence*, 19–41; Doc Childre and Howard Martin, *The HeartMath Solution*, pages 3–23.

20   James Clear, "How Long Does It Actually Take to Form a New Habit? (Backed by Science)," *Huffington Post*, April 10, 2014, www.huffpost.com/entry/forming-new-habits_b_5104807/.

21   Doc Childre and Deborah Rozman, *Transforming Anxiety* (Oakland, CA: New Harbinger Publications, Inc., 2006), pages 211–224.

22   Heidi Grant Halvorson, "To Succeed, Forget Self-Esteem," *Harvard Business Review*, September 20, 2012, https://hbr.org/2012/09/to-succeed-forget-self-esteem/.

23   This quote is often attributed to Katherine Hepburn.

24   Debora Spar, *Wonder Women* (London: Picador, 2014), pages 246–249.

25   Martha Beck, *The Joy Diet* (New York: Harmony, 2003), pages 7–23.

26   Elizabeth Bernstein, "One Habit to Make You Happier Today," *Wall Street Journal*, May 8, 2017, www.wsj.com/articles/one-habit-to-make-you-happier-today-1494259324/.

27   Jim Loehr, *Stress for Success* (New York: Three Rivers Press, 1997), pages 166–168.

28   Doc Childre and Deborah Rozman, *Transforming Anxiety*, page 56.

29   "Personal and Professional Coach Training," Newfield Network, last modified 2021, https://newfieldnetwork.com/.

30   Hooping Harmony, https://www.youtube.com/user/hoopingharmony/, is a YouTube channel that encompasses everything from how to hula hoop to hula meditations and more.

31   Stephen Covey, *The 7 Habits of Highly Effective People* (New York: Free Press, 2004), pages 146–182.

32   David Allen, *Getting Things Done* (New York: Penguin, 2001), pages 181–190.

33   Bob Dunham, "Who We Are," Institute for Generative Leadership, accessed May 20, 2023, https://generateleadership.com/who-we-are/.

34   Heidi Grant Halvorson, "To Succeed, Forget Self-Esteem," *Harvard Business Review*, September 20, 2012, https://hbr.org/2012/09/to-succeed-forget-self-esteem/.

35   Jennifer Openshaw, "The No. 1 Reason Women Are Not Getting Promoted."

36   Geoffrey Moore, *Crossing the Chasm* (New York: Harper Business, 1994), pages 9–59.

37   Mermer Blakeslee, *A Conversation with Fear* (CreateSpace Independent Publishing Platform, 2016), pages 8–20, 63–75.

38   Staff writer, "Vera Wang Honored for Lifetime Achievement," *Columbus Dispatch*, June 5, 2013, http://www.dispatch.com/story/lifestyle/2013/06/05/vera-wang-honored-for-lifetime/23375983007/.

39   "Leadership Team," General Motors, accessed May 20, 2023, http://www.gm.com/our-company/leadership/corporate-officers.html/.

40   Sheryl Sandberg, *Lean In* (New York: Knopf, 2013), page 71.

41   Carol Dweck, *Mindset*, page 79.

42   Lizz Schumer, "Why Mentoring Matters, and How to Get Started," *New York Times*, September 26, 2018, https://www.nytimes.com/2018/09/26/smarter-living/why-mentoring-matters-how-to-get-started.html/.

43   Brené Brown, *Daring Greatly* (New York: Penguin Group, 2012), pages 15–30.

44   Joel De Luca, *Political Savvy* (Berwyn, PA; Evergreen Business Group, 1999), pages 139–141.

45   Robert Hogan, "Helping Leaders Manage Their Dark Side" (International Coaching Federation, Converge17 Conference, Washington, DC, August 25, 2017).

46   Adam Grant, *Give and Take*, pages 46–54.

47   Sheryl Sandberg, *Lean In*, page 164.

48   Jim Roussin's adaption of Megan Tschannen-Moran, *Trust Matters* (San Francisco: Jossey-Bass, 2004), page 126.

49   Stephen R. Covey, *The 7 Habits of Highly Effective People*, pages 185–203.

50   Newfield Coaching, newfieldnetwork.com. A personal and professional coach training organization.

51   Newfield Coaching.

52   Ed Musselwhite, *FIRO-B: Interpersonal Dimensions: Understanding Your FIRO-B Results* (Washington, DC: Consulting Psychologists Press, 1982), page 8.

53   Ed Musselwhite, *FIRO-B*, page 8.

54   Craig Chappelow and Cindy McCauley, "What Good Feedback Really Looks Like," *Harvard Business Review*, May 13, 2019, http://hbr.org/2019/05/what-good-feedback-really-looks-like/.

55   Natalie Baumgartner, "Millennials and Their Desire for Always-On Feedback," *Achievers*, January 15, 2019, www.achievers.com/blog/millennials-and-their-desire-for-always-on-feedback/.

56   Brian O'Connell, "7 Tips for Managing Younger Workers," *HR Magazine*, August 23, 2021, https://www.shrm.org/hr-today/news/hr-magazine/fall2021/pages/managing-young-workers.aspx/.

57   Neya Thanikachalam, "Women Benefit from Close-Knit Group of Women in Workplace, NU Study Says," *Daily Northwestern*, February 12, 2019, http://dailynorthwestern.com/2019/02/12/campus/women-benefit-from-close-knit-group-of-women-in-workplace-nu-study-says/; Brian Uzzi, "Research: Men and Women Need Different Kinds of Networks to Succeed," *Harvard Business Review*, February 25, 2019, http://hbr.org/2019/02/research-men-and-women-need-different-kinds-of-networks-to-succeed/.

58   Olivia Goldhill, "Psychologists Have Identified a Very Good Reason Why Unsolicited Advice Is So Annoying," *Quartz*, May 21, 2018, http://qz.com/1283861/psychologists-have-identified-a-very-good-reason-why-unsolicited-advice-is-so-annoying/.

59   Sylvia Ann Hewlett, *Forget a Mentor, Find a Sponsor* (Brighton, MA: Harvard Business Review Press, 2013).

60   Kathryn Mayer, *Collaborative Competition* (Collaborative Competitive Press, 2009), pages 26–27.

61   Rob Cross, Nitin Nohria, and Andrew Parker, "Six Myths about Informal Networks—and How to Overcome Them," *MIT Sloan Management Review*, April 15, 2002, pages 67-75.

62   Rob Cross and Robert J. Thomas, *Driving Results through Social Networks* (San Francisco: Jossey-Bass, 2008), pages 131–158.

63   Tiziana Casciaro and Miguel Sousa Lobo, "Competent Jerks, Lovable Fools, and the Formation of Social Networks," *Harvard Business Review*, June 2005, http://hbr.org/2005/06/competent-jerks-lovable-fools-and-the-formation-of-social-networks/.

64   Tiziana Casciaro and Miguel Sousa Lobo, "Competent Jerks, Lovable Fools, and the Formation of Social Networks."

65   Mishell Parreno Taylor, "Today's Affinity Groups: Risks and Rewards," *SHRM*, October 11, 2019, www.shrm.org/resourcesandtools/legal-and-compliance/employment-law/pages/affinity-groups-risks-rewards.aspx/.

66   Rob Cross, Nitin Nohria, and Andrew Parker, "Six Myths about Informal Networks—and How to Overcome Them."

67   Gretchen Rubin, *The Happiness Project* (New York: HarperCollins, 2009), page 297.

68   Gretchen Rubin, *The Happiness Project*, page 78.

69 Brené Brown, *Daring Greatly*, pages 15–30.

70 Victoria Castle, *The Trance of Scarcity* (Oakland: Berrett-Koehler, 2007), pages 23–37.

71 Judith A. Waterman and Jenny Rogers, *Introduction to the FIRO-B Instrument* (Washington, DC: Consulting Psychologists Press, 1996), page 2.

72 Sheryl Gay Stolberg, "Shutdown Prompts Centrist Freshman Democrats to Flex Their Muscles," *New York Times*, January 19, 2019, https://www.nytimes.com/2019/01/19/us/politics/freshman-democrats-shutdown-wall.html/.

73 Cinnamon Janzer, "The Truth about Millennial Employees: The Largest Generation in the Workforce," *Workest*, July 23, 2018, http://www.zenefits.com/workest/truth-about-millennials-largest-generation-workforce/; Amy Adkins, "Millennials: The Job-Hopping Generation," *Gallup*, May 12, 2016, http://www.gallup.com/workplace/236474/millennials-job-hopping-generation.aspx/; Dawn Heiberg, "Key Statistics about Millennials in the Workplace," *Firstup*, October 26, 2018, https://firstup.io/blog/key-statistics-millennials-in-the-workplace/.

74 Mermer Blakeslee, *A Conversation with Fear*, pages 155–164.

75 Amy J.C. Cuddy, Matthew Kohut, and John Neffinger, "Connect, Then Lead," *Harvard Business Review*, July-August 2013, pages 3–9.

ACKNOWLEDGMENTS

I feel an immense sense of gratitude that this book became a reality. As a perfectionist, I had already worked on it for several years and had planned to publish it in 2020. Then the pandemic hit. With guidance from several people listed below, I was able to turn the pandemic into a real opportunity to rid myself of some of my perfectionist tendencies and use all the wisdom in this book to keep my sanity and thrive. And luckily, the topic is evergreen.

I am deeply indebted to my marketing/publishing consultant and informal editor, Shel Horowitz, who encouraged me not to give up and help me find the resources to shape this idea. He was the broker who found me many amazing specialists to craft a first-rate product. These included Oshana Himot, who coached me through creating the vision; the second editor, Janice Beetle, who gave this book a very approachable tone and corrected a million grammatical errors; and then Lisa Pelto who hired the perfect person to do the index. Paul Palmer-Edwards created the cover and designed the inside of the book. Your ability to make the typeface enticing and the cover appealing to everyone is amazing!

To all those who participated in my two pilots that led to the creation of this book. Many are former clients, friends, and generous people who brought their full selves, vulnerability, and curiosity to these programs. They participated fully and offered my critical and supportive feedback. These people include: Nancy Cheesman, Elaine Rosenblum, Wendy Tennant-Beebe, Meredith Moore, Anastasia Berezniak, Karen Horting, Susan Posey, Beth Marie O'Laughlin, Tamara Kelly, Michele Durant, Margaret Sherlock, and Michelle Lifschitz.

Doug Leonard, who is an expert in the Birkman Method, generously offered to help me create a risk-taking mindset. He helped me simplify complex topics and made them highly accessible.

There are many people behind the scenes who have played critical roles. To my operations and social media/website team of Kathleen Phelps and Amory King, you both are incredible professionals. I so appreciate your creativity, visual sense, and ability to edit my work so that it entertains and educates. And, to Dasha Dare for her inviting lifestyle photos and Robin Narvaez, my stylist, who ensured I looked like the best version of myself. To my second cousin, Victoria Alicandro, for your assistance in doing some research and writing. Your research helped me score a big-time endorsement! Deborah Hurwitz also did research to identify the top women's employee resource groups (ERG) groups and craft letters to those groups. Ann Minn came up with the brilliant maximum-impact strategy to aim this book towards company Employee Recourse Groups (ERGs) for women. Presentation guru Gary Lyons, a former playwright, actor, singer, and performer extraordinaire, helped me design highly engaging seminars that make the materials in the book come alive!

Thanks to all my clients and supporters who endorsed the book: Dr. Marshall Goldsmith, Dr. Valerie Young, Nicole Clopton, Karen Horting, Tasnim Ghiawadwala, Dr. Rosina Racioppi, Mike Sebring, Susan Posey, Annette Stewart, Leo Giglio, Dr. Tammy Wong, Zhanna Treybick, Bob Dunham, Ann White, Liana Gordon, Anne Weisberg, Priya Kaul, and Margaret Downs. Your support and enthusiasm helped calm my own ever-present doubts. I so appreciate your willingness to take the time to read the book and encourage others to read it! Billie Jean King inspires me on many levels. Her quote, "Pressure is a Privilege," continues to build my courage when I need it most.

Special thanks to two members of my coaching mind master group whom I met with monthly while writing. Marie Dumas came up with the first part of the title – The Productive Perfectionist! I thought that title seemed so boring and yet my editor Shel, rounded out the title to make it catchy! And Ann Parks has been my mentor for over twenty years. You saw and appreciated my creativity in a way that made me value myself more.

Many organizations and companies have supported this work. First and foremost, Susan Posey, Vice President at JPMorgan, who leads Lead the Global Technology Women's initiative supporting the development, retention, and advancement of women in technology. She was willing to pilot the program as I was writing the book in 2019. The International Coaching Federation (ICF) NYC chapter former Presidents Margaret McLean Walsh and Amy Bloustine invited me to deliver a pilot in 2019 while I was finishing up the book. Women's Bond Club, board member Nicole Clopton invited me in December of 2023 to deliver my first book talk before it was finalized. And the Financial Women's Association (FWA) supported a pilot program for college students in March of 2024. The current president of the FWA, Annette Stewart, and Olga Barskaya, who runs the FWA's mentoring program, provided ongoing support. Beth Larrabee of the Career Center of my alma mater, St. Lawrence University had me give a talk to college students right before the book was published in April 2024.

Finally, thanks to my friends and family members. My developmentally disabled brother Chris and his best friend Arthur, who find it funny to be the worst bowlers ever, remind me why striving for perfection isn't always necessary. My 91-year-old aunt eagerly read the book, shared that she could relate to the stories, and thanked me for helping her be a little kinder to herself. My good friends Anne Weisberg and her husband PD Villarreal, Beth

Marie O'Laughlin, Vanessa Palmer, Jeanne Golly, Mike and Marcus Sebring, Debbie Zeigler, and Ellen Perlstein for their ongoing encouragement. Last and most importantly, my dear husband Stuart Diamond gave unwavering support and humor, keeping me laughing even when I thought it wasn't possible.

INDEX

ABOUT KATHRYN MAYER

Kathryn Mayer speaks, writes, coaches, trains, and consults on leadership development. Building on a 30-year career as a talent management executive, facilitator, motivational speaker, and executive coach, Kathryn helps leaders play their biggest and best game, navigate change, lead teams, and build healthy, diverse, and effective organizations.

Kathryn's perspective on leadership is shaped by her experiences as both a former top-ranked amateur tennis player and a Human Resources executive who led change and developed talent in competitive corporate environments, including Goldman Sachs, Deloitte, and Citigroup's investment bank.

Kathryn has helped a wide range of people achieve their dreams. With her coaching, her clients have become Managing Directors in large banks, Partners in consulting firms, and C-Suite executives. They've learned how to thrive through mergers & acquisitions, promotions, and demotions while staying authentic and maintaining choice.

Her two previous books: *Collaborative Competition™: A Woman's Guide to Succeeding by Competing* (2009) and an eBook, *How to Stay SANE and Successful in the COVID World* (2021) received wide acclaim. Her blog at https://www.kcmayer.com/ helps perfectionists-in-recovery (like herself) who strive for excellence and want to enjoy life.

She's also a Newfield Certified Coach and earned her Professional Certified Coach designation from the International Coaching Federation.

Kathryn received a BA in Sociology with Phi Beta Kappa honors from St. Lawrence University and earned an MS in Counseling Psychology from SUNY at Albany. She received the Sol Feinstone Award for Humanitarian Service from St. Lawrence University for her work with Women's World Banking.

Unlock Your Full Productive Potential!

Ready to break free from perfection paralysis and elevate your productivity game? Want to stop sabotaging yourself, smash the shackles of perfectionist paralysis, and turn your blockages into productive perfectionism? Kathryn Mayer, President & Founder of KC Mayer Consulting, Inc., acclaimed coach/presenter, and author of three books including this one, is ready to guide you through your transformative journey. You can choose to do this as part of a group within your organization, a more broad-based cohort, or just you and Kathryn. Kathryn's insightful coaching will help you embrace productivity, innovation, and joy, either as an individual or as part of a team.

Here's what Kathryn can do for you:

- **Individual Coaching**: Tailored six-month to one-year-coaching program to unlock your potential and navigate challenges.

- **Corporate programs**: Elevate your company's productivity and innovation with customized workshops and coaching programs.

- **Women's Leadership development programs**: Increase the number of women who can take charge of their careers and develop new ways of working and stronger networks that will help them grow their careers.

- **Inspirational, action-focused speaking**: Book Kathryn for impactful talks that motivate and drive positive change.

How to get in touch
Please schedule a complimentary 30-minute conversation to learn more: https://www.kcmayer.com/contact-productive-perfectionist

- https://www.kcmayer.com

- LinkedIn https://linkedin.com/in/kathryncmayer/

- Facebook https://facebook.com/KCMConsulting

- Twitter (X) https://twitter.com/GrandslamCoach

Join the Productive Perfectionist support and discussion community!
Kathryn has set up a new community on LinkedIn where you can discuss issues and solutions with your peers and sometimes get advice from Kathryn herself. This will be a moderated discussion group so you can know you're in a safe place where attacks will not be posted and trolls will be banned. Please join at https://www.linkedin.com/groups/13029331/

Made in the USA
Middletown, DE
12 September 2024

60396984R00139